## A Special Note to Mom

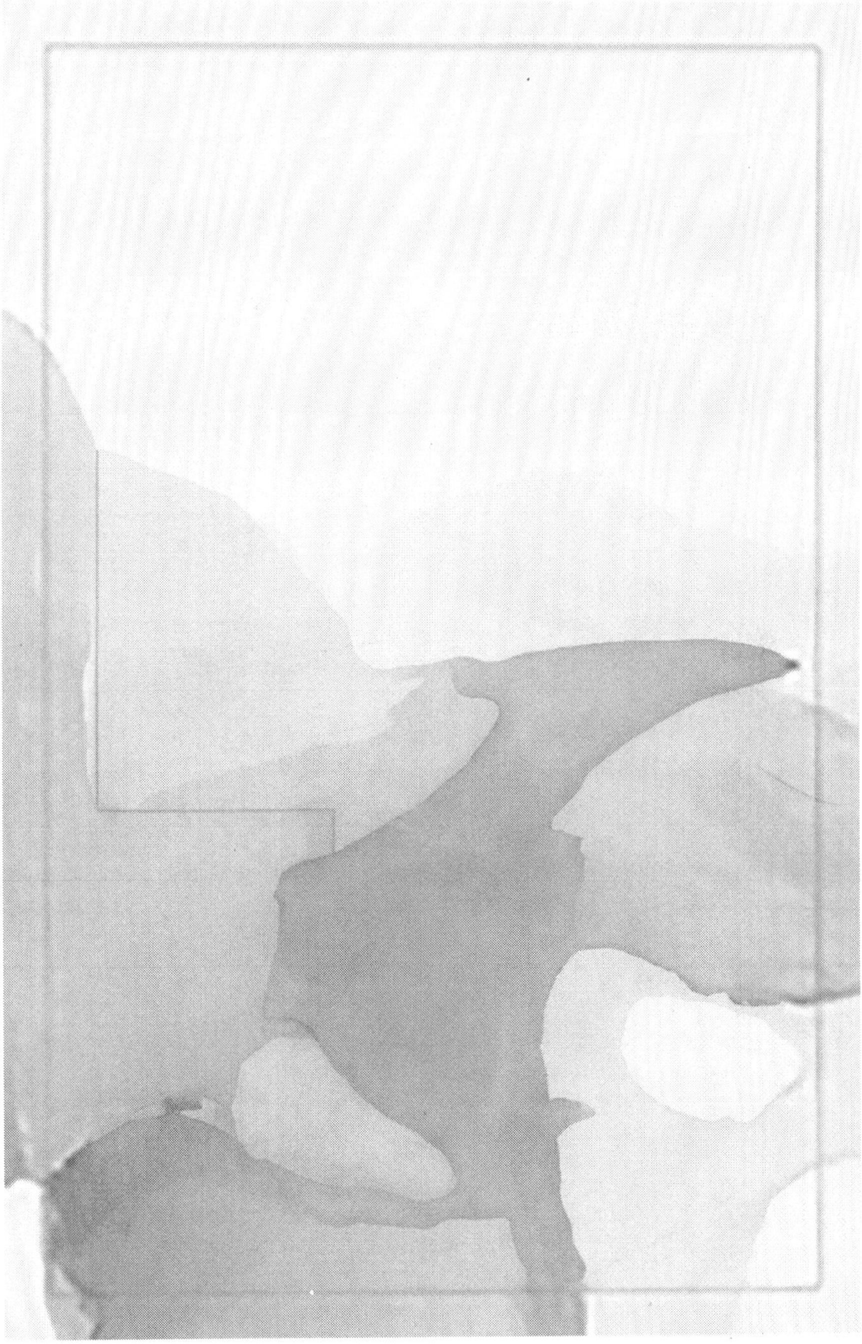

# WHISPERS TO MOM

A COLLECTION OF POEMS CELEBRATING LOVE, RESILIENCE, AND MOTHERS

WHISPERS OF FAMILY SERIES
BOOK 1

## A. PERKINS

AVOY PUBLISHING

Copyright © 2025 by AVOY Publishing

All rights reserved.

No part of this publication may be reproduced, stored, or transmitted in any form or by any means, electronic, mechanical, photocopying, recording, scanning, or otherwise, without written permission from the publisher. It is illegal to copy this book, post it to a website, or distribute it by any other means without permission.

AVOY Publishing has no responsibility for the persistence or accuracy of URLs for external or third-party Internet Websites referred to in this publication and does not guarantee that any content on such Websites is, or will remain, accurate or appropriate.

# AUTHOR'S OTHER WORKS

*Poetry*

- Whispers of Love & Life, A Poetry Collection on Love, Longing, and the Art of Living.
- Whispers of Love & Life, A Poetry Collection on Love, Longing, and the Art of Living. - Part 2
- Whispers of Love & Life, A Poetry Collection on Love, Longing, and the Art of Living. - Part 3
- Beyond the Vail: An Awakening, A Collection of Poetry on A Journey of Growth, Light, and the Unknown
- *The Echo Within, Finding Peace, Power, and the Light Ahead*
- *21 Bars: Poetry from the Inside, Where words break through walls.*
- *Urban Poetry & Truth, The Echo of the Streets*

*To the readers—may these words find you where you are and meet you where you need them most.*

## ACKNOWLEDGMENTS

With deepest gratitude to my wife, daughters, and son. Your unwavering love, support, and presence have been the constant light on this creative journey. Thank you for inspiring every verse and every moment of reflection.

# CONTENTS

*Preface* — 15
*Introduction* — 17
*What Awaits You in These Pages* — 19

PART I
From Birth to Bond: A Mother's Love — 23

PART II
Love and Gratitude: — 59

PART III
Strength and Sacrifice — 101

PART IV
Life Lessons — 143

PART V
Trying Again — 183

PART VI
Growth and Support: — 219

PART VII
Cultural and Generational Ties — 249

PART VIII
Bonus Poems — 287

1. Closing Thoughts — 315
2. Index of Poems — 317
3. Author's Note — 329
4. About the Author — 331

# PREFACE

**Preface**

Mothers are the heart of humanity—a source of love, resilience, wisdom, and selflessness that transcends generations. From the moment they bring life into the world, their role becomes an indelible part of who we are. Their actions, large and small, weave a tapestry of memories, guidance, and unconditional love that shapes us forever.

This book, **Whispers to Mom**, is a gratitude for mothers' incomparable role. It acknowledges their sacrifices, strength, nurturing spirit, and profound impact on our lives. Every poem within these pages serves as a heartfelt expression—a whisper of appreciation and admiration for the women who show love in its purest form.

Through six thoughtfully curated chapters, this collection captures the many facets of motherhood:

*Preface*

- **From Birth to Bond:** A tribute to the miraculous beginnings of life and the enduring connection formed in those earliest years.

- **Strength and Sacrifice:** Honoring the resilience and selflessness that define mothers.

- **Life Lessons:** Reflecting on the wisdom and guidance passed down from mother to child.

- **Memories and Moments:** Celebrating cherished experiences shared with moms.

- **Growth and Support:** Highlighting a mother's role in empowering and uplifting.

- **Cultural and Generational Ties:** Exploring the traditions and heritage mothers preserve across generations.

This book is not merely a collection of poems; it is a tribute, a celebration, and a keepsake. It is a way to say "thank you" in words that often remain unspoken. To the reader, may this book inspire you to reflect on the mothers in your life and our incredible bond.

Whether gifted to your own mom or read in quiet reflection, **Whispers to Mom** serves as a bridge between hearts, connecting us to the love that sustains us.

With heartfelt gratitude, we dedicate this collection to mothers everywhere.

# INTRODUCTION

A mother's love is a force like no other—boundless, enduring, and transformative. It is the foundation of our first breaths, the guide through our milestones, and the unwavering light that carries us through life's darkest moments. **Whispers to Mom** is a celebration of this extraordinary bond, a testament to the strength, grace, and sacrifices that define motherhood.

This collection of poems takes you on a heartfelt journey through the many facets of a mother's love. Each chapter reveals mothers' profound and tender roles—from the life-giving moments of childbirth to the cherished memories and lessons they leave behind. Through their resilience, nurturing support, and ability to connect generations, mothers shape our world with an irreplaceable influence.

*Introduction*

**The opening chapter, From Birth to Bond: A Mother's Love**, reflects on the miraculous beginnings of life and the unbreakable bond formed in those early years. As the pages unfold, each subsequent chapter delves into themes of love, gratitude, strength, cultural heritage, and the timeless wisdom passed through generations. Every poem is a whisper of appreciation and recognition, a voice speaking directly from the heart to the remarkable women who shape our lives.

Whether you are a child honoring your mother or someone reflecting on the universal beauty of motherhood, **Whispers to Mom** offers solace, inspiration, and a way to say the words that often go unsaid. With space for a personal note, this book becomes more than a gift—it becomes a keepsake, a memory, and a timeless expression of love.

To the mothers who give tirelessly, to the children who seek to honor them, and to all who celebrate the essence of motherhood—this book is for you.

# WHAT AWAITS YOU IN THESE PAGES

**This book is divided into seven distinct sections**, each capturing a unique facet of motherhood, love, and life:

### Part 1: From Birth to Bond: A Mother's Love

This section begins with the miraculous moments of childbirth and the nurturing bond formed in the early years. Through heartfelt poems, it celebrates the strength, devotion, and transformative journey of motherhood as life begins.

### Part 2: Love and Gratitude

This is a heartfelt tribute to the immense love and appreciation we hold for mothers. This section is filled with poems expressing our deep gratitude and affection for the women who give us everything, often without asking for anything in return.

**Part 3: Strength and Sacrifice**

This section honors the resilience and sacrifices that mothers make every day. Through touching verses, it reflects on the courage, selflessness, and enduring strength that define a mother's heart, even in life's most challenging moments.

**Part 4: Life Lessons**

Mothers are our first teachers, and this section reflects on their wisdom. Each poem captures the guidance, advice, and nurturing care mothers provide, shaping the character and values of their children.

**Part 5: Trying Again**

This section speaks to perseverance, resilience, and the courage to keep moving forward. It reflects on the moments when mothers inspire us to rise after every fall and to try again, no matter the obstacles.

**Part 6: Growth and Support**

This section highlights how mothers empower and uplift their children. Through heartfelt verses, it honors the encouragement, love, and steadfast support that help us grow into who we are meant to be.

**Part 7: Cultural and Generational Ties**

Mothers serve as bridges between generations, carrying the traditions and heritage that connect families. This section celebrates the cultural bonds and values mothers pass down, preserving our history and unity across time.

**Part 8: Bonus section** Click here.

**For a complete Index of all Poems.** Now, let's turn the page and begin.

## PART I

# FROM BIRTH TO BOND: A MOTHER'S LOVE

This opening section is a heartfelt ode to the miraculous journey of motherhood, beginning with the gift of life itself. It explores the profound, transformative moments of childbirth and the nurturing bond that blooms in the earliest years. Through evocative poems, this chapter honors the love that flows from a mother's heart as she cradles, protects, and watches her child grow.

From the first cry to the first step, every verse captures the essence of a mother's unwavering devotion. It celebrates the sleepless nights, the gentle guidance, and the deep connection that defines this extraordinary bond. These poems reflect the beauty of life's beginnings and the unbreakable ties forged during the tender years.

# 1

## THE MOMENT YOU ARRIVED

When you gave life, the world stood still, A moment of love, beyond all will. Through joy and pain, you brought forth light, A beacon strong, a guiding sight.

With tiny hands and soulful cries, You taught me love that never dies. The bond began, forever true, Through all of life, because of you.

## 2

## THROUGH TENDER YEARS

I watched you nurture, year by year, Through laughter bright and love sincere. Your caring hands, your knowing heart, From life's first step, you played your part.

You held me close, you set me free, A mother's love, pure melody. Through all the lessons, joys, and fears, You shaped my soul through tender years.

## 3

## THE FIRST EMBRACE

Your arms became my safest place, A quiet world, a soft embrace. No words were said, yet I just knew— My every breath belonged to you.

## 4

## WHEN YOU SAID MY NAME

The first time that you called me near, Your voice was calm, your meaning clear. You said my name with tender pride, And something sparked and bloomed inside.

In that small word, your whole heart came— The world grew different with my name.

## 5

## MY FIRST TEACHER

You taught me how to hold a spoon, To hum a tune, to chase the moon. You showed me where the flowers grew, And why the sky could change its hue.

You taught me more than words could say— How love can guide a life each day.

## 6

## THE LANGUAGE OF TOUCH

Before I knew the shape of sound, Your fingertips would wrap around. They told me things no speech could say— That I was safe in every way.

Your hands became my first true guide, Where all my tiny fears would hide.

## 7

## YOUR VOICE WAS MY FIRST SONG

Before I ever knew a word, Your lullabies were all I heard. Soft melodies that filled the air, A mother's love in every prayer.

You didn't need to sing it right— You soothed the dark, you shaped the night. And though the years have stretched and flown, Your song still plays beneath my own.

## 8

## MORNING MOMENTS

Each morning held a quiet grace, The sun would find your peaceful face. You'd hum a tune and stroke my hair, And all my fears dissolved right there.

You brewed the day with gentle care, Your love was light, your warmth was air. In every sip of morning tea, You passed your calm and peace to me.

## 9

# HELD WITHOUT ASKING

There were no words, no cries, no call, You simply knew—I'd start to fall. And in that instant, without sound, Your arms were there to wrap around.

No questions asked, no need to prove, Your comfort always made me move. In every stumble, large or small, You taught me not to fear the fall.

## 10

## YOU NAMED ME TWICE

You named me once when I was born, And once again in every morn. With nicknames sweet, and silly too, Each name a thread that pulled me through.

In every word, your love would gleam, You spoke my soul into a dream. And now I name you just the same— With every whisper of your name.

## 11

## A MOTHER'S HANDS

Your hands, not fine, not trimmed or fair, But full of life and love and care. They brushed my brow, they tied my shoes, They taught me how to win—and lose.

With every touch, a lesson laid, Of all the sacrifices made. Your hands, though worn, were always sure— A silent strength that would endure.

## 12

# THE BLANKET YOU WOVE

You made a blanket, stitch by stitch, Not from yarn, but love that's rich. Each patch a prayer, each thread a vow, To hold me then and hold me now.

It wasn't made with thread or seam— It wrapped my heart, it shaped my dream. And though it's gone, I still feel warm, Within the fabric of your arms.

## 13

# THROUGH FEVERED NIGHTS

You sat beside me through the heat, With quiet hands and whispered feet. No rest for you, no sleep, no sigh— Just steady love when I would cry.

The medicine you gave was time, A lullaby, a soft-spoke rhyme. And in the haze of pain and fear, You stayed until the light drew near.

## 14

# THE FIRST GOODBYE

The day you let me walk away, To face the world, to find my way— You smiled through tears and kissed my hair, Pretending you were fine right there.

But I could feel the silent ache, The way your heart began to break. Still, you stood tall and let me roam, And left the porch light on at home.

## 15

## YOU WERE MY WORLD

The house was small, the days were long, But you made magic all along. A cardboard box became a boat, And lullabies would gently float.

You were the center of my skies, The one who wiped my teary eyes. Before I knew the world was wide— I had it all with you inside.

## 16

# THE FIRST TIME YOU PRAYED FOR ME

Your whispered words were soft and low, Too quiet for the world to know. But in the hush, a vow was made— A mother's heart that humbly prayed.

You didn't ask for wealth or fame, Just strength to guide me through the flame. You gave me faith with every plea, And wrapped the future carefully.

Though time may shift and seasons flee, I still feel safe—you prayed for me.

## 17

# A CRADLE OF LIGHT

You wrapped me in more than a sheet, You wrapped me in a warmth complete. The night was deep, the world unsure— But you became my quiet cure.

Your touch, a soft and glowing thread, Lit every shadow round my bed. No nightlight could compete with you— The way you made the dark feel new.

And though I've long since outgrown size, You're still the light behind my eyes.

## 18

## THE SONGS YOU MADE UP

You made up songs no one would hear, But somehow they would draw me near. A jumbled tune, a playful rhyme, The music marking sacred time.

They didn't have a perfect verse, Yet they would heal what once felt worse. Each silly word, each lilt and hum, Would tell me brighter days would come.

Those made-up songs, so wild, so true— Were love in melody from you.

## 19

## THE LESSONS IN THE SMALL THINGS

You taught me more through simple deeds— To water roots, to plant the seeds. To sweep the floor with patient grace, And wipe the worries from your face.

The little things became so grand, When done with heart and gentle hand. I didn't know then what you gave— A map for how I should behave.

Now I see, in every chore— You taught me life, and something more.

## 20

# ALWAYS THE FIRST TO SEE

You saw my gifts before I knew, Believed in things I couldn't do. Your faith in me became my wings— You saw the good in broken things.

Before the crowd would cheer or scorn, You knew what I was made for, born. You were the mirror, kind and clear, That showed me all I hold most dear.

And still today, in all I be— You're always first—the one to see.

## 21

## THE MOMENT YOU ARRIVED

When you gave life, the world stood still, A moment of love, beyond all will. Through joy and pain, you brought forth light, A beacon strong, a guiding sight.

With tiny hands and soulful cries, You taught me love that never dies. The bond began, forever true, Through all of life, because of you.

## 22

# THE WAY YOU LOOKED AT ME

Before I spoke a single word, You understood and always heard. You saw the truth within my eyes, And soothed my fears before my cries.

The way you looked at me that day— It said, "I love you. Come what may."

## 23

# THROUGH TENDER YEARS

I watched you nurture, year by year, Through laughter bright and love sincere. Your caring hands, your knowing heart, From life's first step, you played your part.

You held me close, you set me free, A mother's love, pure melody. Through all the lessons, joys, and fears, You shaped my soul through tender years.

## 24

## THE STRENGTH YOU SHOWED

I saw your strength when life began, Through sacred trials, through human span. Your courage vast, your purpose clear, You faced the world without a fear.

The cries that marked the birth of me, Were echoes of your bravery. Each act you did, each step you sowed, I'll always honor the strength you showed.

## 25

## LIFE'S FIRST GIFT

You gave a gift no words could name, A love that burned a steady flame. Through pain endured and dreams let fly, You built my world beneath the sky.

Your hands that held, your gentle grace, Forever stay my sacred place.

## 26

## THE BOND YOU MADE

A bond was forged in love's first glow, A tie that time cannot outgrow. You gave me strength, you gave me care, A mother's love beyond compare.

Through every step, through every fall, You were my guide, my all in all.

## 27

# A THOUSAND LULLABIES

You sang to me through sleepless nights, With whispered songs and dimmed-down lights. Your voice—a balm, so sweet and low— Taught me more than you could know.

Each lullaby, a vow so deep, That you'd love me through every leap.

## 28

## CRADLED IN LOVE

Cradled in love's warm embrace, You showed me life's own gentle face. Through sleepless nights and days of cheer, Your love was constant, always near.

Your love endures a soft refrain, A steady balm through joy and pain.

## 29

# IN THE QUIET MOMENTS

In quiet moments, late at night, You whispered love without the light. No grand display, no need for show— Just steady love that let me grow.

Those silences still hold me tight, Like echoes wrapped in mysteries light.

## 30

# ROCKED IN YOUR ARMS

Rocked in your arms, the world stood still, A cradle soft against life's chill. The rhythm of your heart and song Told me where I would belong.

I didn't know what time could steal, But in your arms, I learned to feel.

## 31

## THE FIRST EMBRACE

The first embrace, so soft, so sweet, A mother's touch, where hearts first meet. Through every moment, every care, You gave me love beyond compare.

That gentle hug, a memory bright, Will guide me through my darkest night.

## 32

# YOUR SACRIFICE

You gave so much, your heart, your time, Through sleepless nights and steps to climb. A love so pure, so vast, so true, You built the world I journey through.

Each moment spent, your care ensures, A bond of love that still endures.

## 33

## YOUR ENDLESS LOVE

Your endless love, so vast, so true, Has built the world I journey through. Through every moment, every care, You showed me love beyond compare.

Forever thankful, my soul will be, For all the ways you've nurtured me.

## 34

## THE WAY YOU WATCHED ME SLEEP

You watched me sleep with softened eyes, As if you saw the stars arise. No moment rushed, no task ahead— Just quiet love around my bed.

I never knew the peace you gave Until I missed the way you'd stay. Now every dream I drift into Still carries traces wrapped in you.

# PART II

# LOVE AND GRATITUDE:

This section is a heartfelt celebration of our immense love and appreciation for mothers. Through tender and evocative poems, it reflects our gratitude for their endless sacrifices, unconditional care, and profound impact on our lives.

Mothers give without measure, often in ways unseen, yet their love remains the backbone of every cherished moment and every life lesson. **Love and Gratitude** honor this devotion, serving as a reminder to thank them for all the gifts they offer. Whether in small, everyday acts or grand gestures, a mother's love is unparalleled, and this chapter captures the essence of that appreciation.

These poems invite readers to reflect on the countless ways mothers shape us, inspire us, and empower us.

## 35

## A HEART THAT GAVE WITHOUT RETURN

You gave without the need to gain, Through sleepless nights and quiet pain. You didn't ask for grand displays, Just love returned in simple ways.

And now I see, with older eyes, The silent ways you made me rise. A life you built from dreams you burned— A heart that gave without return.

## 36

## THANK YOU FOR STAYING

When storms rolled in, you didn't leave, You stood your ground, you let me grieve. You stayed through chaos, through my mess, With love that asked for nothing less.

So now I say what's long been due— Thank you, Mom, for being you.

## 37

## I DIDN'T KNOW THEN

I didn't know how hard it was To give with grace and never pause. To wear a smile when days were long, To stay so soft and still be strong.

But now I see through clearer glass— You loved me most when strength would pass.

## 38

## THE MEALS YOU MADE

You fed us more than food alone, You fed us love in every tone. Each plate a gift, each bite a hug, Each stew and soup, a warm heart snug.

We didn't say it then out loud— But every meal made you more proud.

## 39

## A QUIET THANK YOU

I didn't always say the words, Too caught in days, too full of blur. But every act, each thoughtful deed, Fulfilled a deeply rooted need.

So here's my thanks, though late it came— You gave me love without a name.

## 40

## YOU CLAPPED THE LOUDEST

You cheered for me when I was small, And even when I'd slip or fall. Your voice would rise above the crowd, Unshaken, steady, warm, and loud.

No matter what I dared to try— You clapped the loudest, standing by.

## 41

# THE NOTES YOU WROTE

A lunchbox note, a scribbled line, A drawing done in pen and twine. I kept them tucked inside my chest— The parts of you I loved the best.

They weren't long poems or letters grand, But little sparks from your sweet hand.

## 42

## I KNOW NOW WHAT IT COST

Each gift you gave, each role you played, Was bought with nights you never stayed. With dreams delayed and plans unseen— So I could have a brighter scene.

I didn't know, but now I do— The price of love was paid by you.

## 43

## YOUR LOVE WAS LOUD WITHOUT A SOUND

You didn't shout what you had done, You simply showed up, one by one. From laundry folded, socks aligned, To birthday cakes so sweetly timed.

Your love was loud in subtle ways— It filled the cracks of all my days.

## 44

## WHEN I FORGOT TO SAY IT

There were days I moved too fast, Moments when your love flew past. But even when I lost my way, You stayed, though I forgot to say.

So now I pause, I look, I write— To say I see you. Clear as light.

## 45

## YOU GAVE ME YOUR MORNINGS

You rose before the sun could shine, To pack my lunch and check the time. With sleepy eyes and steady grace, You sent me off to find my place.

You never asked for praise or pay, Just smiled and waved me on my way. And now I see those simple starts Were how you poured out all your heart.

## 46

## THE HANDS THAT HELD MY WORLD

Your hands were firm, yet soft with care, They tied my shoes, they brushed my hair. They carried dreams and wiped my tears, And held me close through all the years.

Those hands were tired, sometimes worn, But never once did they feel torn. With every touch, they left their trace— A gentle strength, a quiet grace.

## 47

## A THANK YOU LEFT UNSAID

I should have said it more, I know— How much your love helped me to grow. But youth moves fast and pride runs deep, And some things silence tries to keep.

Still, every act and every smile Was logged in me across each mile. And now I speak with open thread— A thank you once left still unsaid.

## 48

## YOUR LOVE WAS IN THE DETAILS

In folded clothes and cleaned-up shoes, In birthday cards with handpicked hues, In school supplies and measured books, In knowing glances, patient looks—

Your love lived in the quiet things, Not roses red or diamond rings. But acts that bloomed with every day— In all the ways you paved my way.

## 49

## WHEN YOU LET ME GO

You knew the day would surely come When I would leave the place I'm from. You packed my bags with all your care, And slipped a note to leave me there.

You smiled, but tears welled up inside, A mother's strength, a softer pride. And in that parting, full and slow, I felt how hard it was... to let me go.

## 50

## ALL THE THINGS I NEVER NOTICED

The bills you paid, the socks you mended, The silent ways your patience blended. The plans you changed so I could grow— Those things I never saw or know.

But now, I trace them in my mind, The hidden gifts you left behind. Each one a thread in love's design— Proof you were never far from mine.

## 51

## YOUR VOICE WAS ALWAYS NEAR

I hear it now in quiet rooms, In gentle winds or whispered tunes. Your voice, though soft, was always near— A steady echo year to year.

In words you said a thousand times, In bedtime talks and silly rhymes. I find your voice in all I do— It still says, "I believe in you."

## 52

# I KNOW NOW WHY YOU WAITED

You sat outside my dance class doors, Through soccer games and grocery stores. You waited, silent, rain or shine— As if your time was always mine.

I didn't see how much it took, To stop your world and just let me look. But now I do—and with full view— I'd wait forever, just like you.

## 53

## THE GIFTS YOU DIDN'T WRAP

The gifts you gave were never tied With fancy bows or paper wide. They came in form of time and care, Of meals and hugs and answered prayers.

You didn't need a holiday To give your love in quiet ways. The gifts you gave still hold their light— A mother's touch, forever right.

## 54

## THE THANK YOU IN MY EYES

I never said the words enough, For all your fierce and tender stuff. But in my gaze, I hope you see The gratitude you gave to me.

It lives in how I walk today, In how I love, in what I say. So though my lips may not have tried— The thank you lives within my eyes.

## 55

# THE STRENGTH BEHIND THE SMILE

You smiled when things were falling through, When no one knew what you'd been through. You faced the storms with lifted chin, And never let the dark win in.

You bore the weight behind closed doors, And still gave more, and more, and more. While others saw a calm disguise, I later found the fire inside.

That smile, it wasn't weakness worn— It was the strength in which I'm born.

## 56

## CARRYING MORE THAN YOU SHARED

You carried loads I couldn't see, While leaving all the light for me. I thought your calm was simply grace— But now I know that wasn't the case.

You held back tears so I could smile, You stood alone and walked each mile. And in your silence, fierce and wide, You made the room feel safe inside.

The things you bore, you never aired— You carried more than you ever shared.

## 57

## THE SLEEPLESS YEARS

You gave up sleep without regret, And never once did you forget. To hush my cries, to soothe my head, To kiss my brow and make my bed.

Through fevered nights and baby sighs, You walked the halls with tired eyes. And though you longed to close your own, You stayed until the dark was gone.

I rest today on love like yours— A mother's strength that still endures.

## 58

# THE FIRE IN YOUR FIGHT

You fought for me when I was small, In ways I didn't see at all. You battled bills and biting cold, And still made magic, brave and bold.

Not with fists or shouted pride, But in the ways you stood and tried. You taught me how to rise with grace, To fight with heart and still embrace.

Your love was fire, your will was steel— A silent force I still can feel.

## 59

## YOU BROKE SO I COULD HEAL

You bent beneath the weight of years, And took my burdens, dried my tears. You cracked in silence, lost your sleep, So I could stand and dream and leap.

You wore your wounds behind a smile, Walked through storms and every trial. Not once did you let go of me— You stayed through pain I couldn't see.

I rise today, because you kneeled— You broke so I could learn to heal.

## 60

## A MOTHER'S LOVE

Your tender touch, a calming embrace, A beacon of warmth, a sacred space. Through sleepless nights and weary days, Your love shines bright in endless ways.

Your voice so soothing, your heart so true, In all life's storms, we lean on you. Your laughter, your wisdom, your guiding light, Turns the darkest moments into bright.

From gentle whispers to heartfelt cheers, You calm our worries and ease our fears. No bond on earth could ever compare, To a mother's love, beyond all care.

Forever cherished, your love profound, Your strength and grace always unbound. For a mother's heart is the purest treasure, A gift of love, beyond all measure.

## 61

# THE HEART THAT ALWAYS KNOWS

Your heart, a compass guiding me, Through life's vast storms, across the sea. Each whispered word, each gentle touch, Speaks of love, a bond so much.

You hold me close when skies are gray, And brighten up my darkest day. A mother's love, both firm and kind, The strongest force you'll ever find.

Through joys and sorrows, highs and lows, You're the heart that always knows.

## 62

## YOUR GENTLE LIGHT

In your arms, the world feels whole, A haven built with heart and soul. You guide with love, through joy and pain, Your gentle light, a sweet refrain.

A smile that warms, a hand so strong, A melody where we belong. Through every storm, you stay the course, A mother's love, an endless source.

With every step, your love remains, Through sunshine bright, and shadowed rains. Forever cherished, your gift divine, A bond eternal, yours and mine.

## 63

# THE BOND YOU BUILD

You nurture dreams and guide the way, With love that lights each passing day. A fortress strong, a heart so pure, Through every trial, your love endures.

Your whispers calm, your laughter heals, Your tender care, a warmth that feels. Each gentle hug, each spoken word, A bond eternal, deeply stirred.

## 64

## THE KEEPER OF DREAMS

You cradle hope and guard the skies, With love that sees through weary eyes. A keeper of dreams, a treasure rare, A mother's heart beyond compare.

Through endless nights and tireless days, Your love endures, in countless ways. Forever cherished, a gift supreme, You are the keeper of every dream.

## 65

## FOREVER YOUR SONG

Your lullaby, a soft refrain, A melody to soothe the pain. Through laughter bright and shadows long, Your love remains forever my song.

No sweeter tune the world can hear, Than the voice of a mother near.

## 66

## BEACON OF LOVE

When storms arise and skies turn gray, Your love becomes the guiding ray. A lighthouse bold, through waters wide, With you, there's nothing left to hide.

Each word, each glance, a soothing balm, In your embrace, the world feels calm.

## 67

## YOU TAUGHT ME HOW

You taught me how to rise and stand, To reach for dreams with steady hand. With every lesson, your heart would show, The seeds of strength you'd help me grow.

Your wisdom lingers in all I do, A mother's gift, forever true.

## 68

## YOUR GENTLE WAYS

The way you smile, the way you heal, Your tender heart, your will of steel. A mother's love, so softly shared, A treasure vast, beyond compared.

Through every step, through every phase, I'm thankful for your gentle ways.

## 69

## THE ROOTS YOU LAY

With every step, the roots you lay, Keep me grounded, guide my way. A sturdy bond, both strong and true, Forever I'll give thanks to you.

Your love, the soil where dreams can grow, The greatest gift I'll ever know.

## 70

## RADIANT SOUL

Your soul is radiant, warm, and kind, A brighter light, I'll never find. Each action speaks of love so pure, Through every test, your care endures.

Forever cherished, your heart's sweet role, A mother's love, a radiant soul.

# 71

## YOU ARE MY ANCHOR

Through shifting tides and oceans wide, You've been my anchor, steady inside. A mother's love, a port in the storm, Through all life's chaos, you keep me warm.

Your strength and care, my heart's delight, An anchor firm, in day or night.

## 72

## TIMELESS LOVE

Your love transcends both time and space, A boundless gift, a warm embrace. Through every stage, through every year, Your heart remains forever near.

A mother's love, so vast, so free, A timeless bond, for all to see.

## 73

## SHELTER FROM THE STORM

When winds would howl and shadows grew, Your love, the shelter I turned to. A fortress strong, a calming grace, Your arms, a warm and sacred place.

Through every storm, I've come to see, Your love will always shelter me.

## 74

## UNBREAKABLE BOND

The bond we share, a golden thread, Through life's vast journey, gently led. A love unbreakable, built to last, Through present trials, future, and past.

# PART III

# STRENGTH AND SACRIFICE

This section is a tribute to the unwavering strength and selflessness that define motherhood. Through deeply touching poems, it explores the quiet courage mothers display daily, often without recognition, as they face life's challenges with resilience and determination.

Mothers carry the world's weight while shielding their loved ones from its burdens. They put their children's needs above their own, often making sacrifices to ensure their families thrive. **Strength and Sacrifice** honors these acts of love and bravery, shedding light on the sacrifices that build the foundation of a child's life and future.

These verses invite readers to reflect on mothers' silent acts of heroism—.

## 75

# THE HANDS THAT DIDN'T TREMBLE

When life grew loud and walls would shake, You held it all for my own sake. Your hands stayed calm, your voice stayed low, While chaos had no place to go.

You mended wounds you didn't cause, You moved with grace, you never paused. Through every ache you didn't show— You stayed, so I would never know.

Those hands that bore what I outgrew, Never trembled— only grew.

## 76

# THE DAY YOU WENT WITHOUT

You passed the plate and watched me eat, While hiding hunger at your seat. You smiled and said, "I'm full today," But silence gave your truth away.

You missed your turn to make me shine, You gave up dreams so I had mine. And never once did you complain, You simply bore the joy and strain.

Now every gift I hold with grace— I see the hunger in your place.

## 77

## QUIET DOESN'T MEAN WEAK

You didn't need to raise your voice, To lead with strength or make a choice. Your calm became the steadiest sound, That kept our feet upon the ground.

While others roared to claim control, You ruled with love and gave me soul. You showed me how to bend, not break, To hold my truth, and never fake.

You proved what strength is meant to be— In quiet acts of dignity.

## 78

## YOU NEVER LEFT THE ROOM

When I would cry without a clue, You simply stayed and sat right through. No lecture came, no big display— Just presence that refused to stray.

You let me feel, you let me fall, And helped me stand up through it all. No judgment passed, no need to roam— You made my sorrow feel like home.

Your love was strong because it stayed, When most would leave, you gently stayed.

## 79

# THE SACRIFICE I NEVER SAW

You stood behind while I took flight, And kissed me every single night. You dimmed your dreams so mine could grow, And smiled through things I'll never know.

You cut corners I couldn't see, So I could move and still be free. And never once did you confess— That all you had, you gave me less.

Now that I see it, every flaw— Was paved by sacrifice I never saw.

## 80

# YOU LOVED ME THROUGH THE HARD PARTS

When I was sharp and full of storm, You loved me still, through every form. You didn't run when I grew cold, You wrapped me close and gently told—

That even when I pulled away, You'd stay beside me anyway. And now I see that kind of grace— It takes a heart the world can't place.

## 81

## THE WAY YOU SOFTENED SUFFERING

You couldn't fix the pain I felt, But stayed beside the hand I dealt. You didn't try to push it through, You simply held the ache I knew.

And in that space, your silence spoke— Of every promise you'd invoke. You didn't need to take it all— You stayed beside, and that was all.

## 82

# THE COST OF LOVING ME

I never asked what love would cost, But now I count what you have lost. The missed ambitions, days alone— The pieces of you overthrown.

And still, you gave without delay, So I could learn, and dream, and play. The cost was great, yet freely given— A mother's love, both worn and driven.

# 83

## THE DAY YOU DIDN'T CRY

You saw me hurt, but didn't weep, You kissed my cheek and let me sleep. I thought your silence meant you missed— But strength was in the things you kissed.

You waited till I couldn't see, Then sobbed for both the pain and me. You didn't cry when I was near— You held the flood behind your fear.

## 84

## YOUR PATIENCE WAS MY SHIELD

When I was loud and lost in fire, You met me with a calm entire. You didn't match my youthful flare, You answered rage with quiet care.

You taught me not to break and burn, But pause and breathe, and wait my turn. I didn't see then what you'd yield— Your patience was my greatest shield.

## 85

## YOU HID YOUR HURTS

You hid your hurts so I could heal, You masked the weight you couldn't feel. You gave me peace while holding pain, And danced beneath the quiet rain.

You whispered hope when yours was gone, And lit my path while losing dawn. Now every joy I carry near— Was built from all you wouldn't fear.

## 86

## YOU CHOSE ME OVER REST

When sleep would call, you still chose me, To hold, to soothe, to gently be. You stayed through midnight's aching hum, Until the light of morning come.

You chose again, and then once more, To give me love you couldn't store. And though you longed for rest, I see— You always stood as my tree.

## 87

## THE SILENCE YOU ENDURED

I gave you grief without a cause, And met your care with teenage pause. But never once did you give in, You held your hurt behind your grin.

You took the silence I would give, And answered it with how you live. And now I see your quiet war— You loved me louder than before.

## 88

## YOU WERE THE ONE WHO STAYED

When others left, or turned away, You were the one who chose to stay. Through broken plans and empty air, You stood with love no one could tear.

You didn't flinch, you didn't move, You only found more ways to prove— That when the world began to fade, You'd still be there. You'd still have stayed.

## 89

# THE FIRE IN YOUR QUIET WAYS

There was no need for grand displays, You fought with fire in quiet ways. You battled storms with steady grace, And kept the peace in every place.

Your strength was not a flashing light— It was the candle in the night. And now, wherever I may roam— Your quiet fire still calls me home.

## 90

## YOU TAUGHT ME RIGHT FROM WRONG

Not from a book or list of rules, But through your life and simple tools. You showed me right in how you gave, And wrong in what you wouldn't save.

You didn't preach or raise your tone, You led by love, by seeds you'd sown. And now I find, through joy or song, I carry what you knew all along.

## 91

## LESSONS IN THE LITTLE THINGS

In brushing teeth and folding clothes, In how to walk with softened toes, You taught me things I didn't see— Like how small acts can set us free.

You made each chore a silent guide, To strength and kindness tucked inside. And every habit that I keep— Was something taught before my sleep.

## 92

## YOU TAUGHT ME HOW TO SPEAK

You showed me when to raise my voice, And when to make a gentler choice. You didn't silence what I felt— But taught me how to pause and dwell.

You shaped my tone, you tamed my fire, You gave my words both wings and wire. And now I speak, both bold and true— Because I first was heard by you.

## 93

## HOW TO LOVE AND LET GO

You held me close, then let me run, And taught me love was never done. It doesn't clutch or hold too tight, It lets us stretch and seek our light.

You smiled through moments hard to bear, And never chained me with your care. From you I learned what real love shows— To love is also to let go.

## 94

## YOU MADE ME APOLOGIZE

You made me say, "I'm sorry," loud, Not out of shame, or for a crowd. But so I'd learn that healing grows In hearts that bend and ego slows.

You didn't scold with cruel demand— You taught me gently, hand in hand. And now I know how peace is made— Because of every time I stayed.

## 95

# THE TRUTH IN YOUR EYES

You told the truth with softened tone, And never left me all alone. You didn't lie to shield the pain, You taught me loss, you named the rain.

Your eyes would say what words could miss— Like when a hug replaced a kiss. And in your truth, I found my grace— A compass drawn from your embrace.

## 96

## YOU TAUGHT ME GRACE IN FAILING

You let me lose, you let me fall, You didn't fix or change it all. You helped me see that pain can grow, That failure isn't just a blow.

You stood beside me, not above, And wrapped my pride with quiet love. Now when I fall, I don't retreat— You taught me grace, not just defeat.

## 97

## HOW TO FORGIVE

You showed me how to bend, not break, To give, even when hearts ache. You let go first, then helped me learn That holding on can also burn.

Forgiveness isn't weakness worn— It's how the strongest hearts are born. I saw you choose it, time again— And taught me mercy through your pain.

## 98

## WHAT MATTERS MOST

You taught me not to chase the gold, But hold the hands I long to hold. To value laughter more than fame, And never fear a smaller name.

You made the quiet life feel bright, And filled the dark with softer light. You showed me how to count the cost— And never lose what matters most.

## 99

# YOU TAUGHT ME TO BE ME

You never shaped me in your mold, Or told me what to chase or hold. You gave me space to dream and be, To grow inside my own strange tree.

You loved me loud, you loved me still, Through every shift of heart and will. And in your eyes, I came to see— The safest thing was being me.

## 100

## THE POWER YOU BEAR

In every storm, you stand so tall, A guiding strength through it all. Your courage shines, a beacon bright, Turning shadows into light.

With every step, your love remains, A steady force through joy and pain.

## 101

## UNSEEN SACRIFICES

The sacrifices that you endure, Silent, unseen, so pure. You give your all, with heart so wide, And in your care, the world resides.

Through every moment, through each mile, You lift us up with every smile.

## 102

## THROUGH TIRELESS NIGHTS

When darkness falls, you stay awake, Your quiet strength, no one can break. Through sleepless nights and endless care, Your love remains beyond compare.

Each sacrifice, each whispered plea, A mother's heart, eternally.

## 103

## THE BURDEN YOU CARRY

You carry burdens not your own, With love so vast, with grace full-grown. Through every heartache, every strife, You give the world a better life.

Your sacrifice, a path so true, The gift of mothers, blessed in you.

## 104

## THE STRENGTH YOU SHOW

Your strength, a rock, a steady hand, Through storms that rise, through shifting sand. You bear the weight, you ease the pain, Your steadfast care, your constant reign.

Each moment proves your love is true, The strength of mothers, found in you.

## 105

## A SHIELD OF LOVE

You shield us from the world's cruel storm, With love so fierce, so pure, so warm. No obstacle can block your way, Your strength endures, day by day.

Through battles fought and trials faced, Your selfless heart cannot be replaced.

## 106

## YOUR QUIET RESOLVE

Through silent tears and whispered prayers, You face the world, despite its snares. Your quiet strength, a force unseen, A love so vast, a heart serene.

Each sacrifice, each moment shared, A mother's love, forever cared.

## 107

## YOUR ENDLESS FIGHT

You fight for those you hold so dear, With endless love, with endless cheer. Through every loss, through every gain, You heal the world's relentless pain.

Your sacrifice, a lasting flame, A mother's strength, forever fame.

## 108

# THE COURAGE TO GIVE

You give your all, no thought to pause, With courage vast and no applause. Through selfless acts and steady care, You love with passion, beyond compare.

Your heart so bold, your strength so true, A mother's love, the rarest view.

## 109

## THE WEIGHT YOU BEAR

You bear the weight of countless needs, With care so vast, with noble deeds. Through every sorrow, every smile, You ease the pain, you walk the mile.

Your strength, a beacon shining bright, A mother's love, a constant light.

## 110

## THROUGH EVERY STRIFE

Through every strife, through every pain, Your strength prevails, your love remains. A guiding force, a steadfast way, Through darkest night and brightest day.

Your sacrifices, vast and true, A mother's gift, a heart in you.

## 111

## STRENGTH UNSEEN

Your strength unseen, a silent force, A mother's care, a steady course. Through endless trials, through skies so gray, You guide us gently on our way.

Your selfless love, your tireless fight, A mother's gift, a shining light.

## 112

## THROUGH EVERY SCAR

Through every scar, through every tear, You face the world, despite the fear. With love so vast, with strength so rare, You guide us gently, always there.

Your heart so kind, your love so pure, A mother's bond that will endure.

## 113

## THE FORCE YOU ARE

A force so steady, firm and kind, A mother's heart, the purest find. Through trials faced and battles fought, You give the love the world has sought.

Your strength, a flame that never dies, A mother's care, a lasting prize.

## PART IV

# LIFE LESSONS

Mothers are our first and most enduring teachers, imparting wisdom that shapes our character and values throughout life. This section reflects on the countless lessons mothers pass down—lessons of kindness, resilience, courage, and love.

Through heartfelt poems, **Life Lessons** captures the quiet guidance and nurturing care that helps us navigate the complexities of life. From teaching us right from wrong to encouraging us to dream and persevere, a mother's influence is immeasurable and everlasting.

These verses honor how mothers empower and inspire us, planting seeds of wisdom that bloom. Whether through their words, actions, or presence, their lessons stay with us.

## 114

## THE POWER OF PLEASE AND THANK YOU

You taught me words that open doors, Not ones from books or distant shores. But small, kind phrases we forget— That make the world a bit more set.

You showed me grace in how you spoke, In every favor, every joke. A thank you soft, a please so true— That's where I learned what words can do.

## 115

## THE LESSONS WEREN'T IN BOOKS

You didn't need a chalk or slate To help me shape my heart or fate. You taught me more through daily deeds— Like tending roots before the weeds.

From folding sheets to baking bread, To hearing pain that went unsaid. I learned from all you chose to do— A thousand truths I hold from you.

## 116

## THE WAY YOU HANDLED ANGER

You didn't scream or walk away, You let your breath lead what you'd say. You didn't slam a single door— You whispered peace, and asked for more.

You showed me storms don't need to roar, That love can wait behind the war. And now when tempers rise in me, I breathe with what you taught to be.

## 117

## YOU TAUGHT ME TIME WAS GOLD

You made the minutes matter most, Not just the parties, gifts, or toast. But bedtime talks and morning light, And walks beneath the stars at night.

You showed me how to waste no day— To see the gift in work and play. You didn't teach with clocks or rhyme— But by the way you spent your time.

## 118

## YOU SHOWED ME HOW TO LISTEN

You listened with your full intent, Not just for words, but what they meant. You didn't fix me right away, You simply stayed and let me say.

You taught me that to truly hear Is standing still and drawing near. And now I offer others grace— Because you held that quiet space.

## 119

## LESSONS IN APPLAUSE

You clapped the loudest when I failed, You smiled when confidence derailed. You didn't cheer for only wins— But showed me where the praise begins.

Applause, you said, should meet the try— Not just the score, the test, the high. And now I clap for others, too— Because I learned that grace from you.

## 120

## YOU LET ME ASK THE QUESTIONS

You never said, "Because I said," Or let the wonder leave my head. You welcomed every why and how, And let me question even now.

You made the world feel wide and kind, And honored every growing mind. Your answers weren't always complete— But every one was pure and sweet.

## 121

## YOU TAUGHT ME TO MAKE DO

When things were tight and life was lean, You turned the plain to something keen. A sweater patched, a toy remade, A feast from scraps you slyly laid.

You didn't pout, you didn't fold— You stitched our lives with thread and gold. And now I find in struggle too— I stand with strength. I make do too.

## 122

# HOW TO APOLOGIZE WITH GRACE

You said, "I'm sorry," when you were wrong, And didn't wait or drag it long. You showed me how the heart can mend, When pride steps back and meets a friend.

You didn't act above or cold— But made humility feel bold. I learned from you that pride may fall— But grace will always rise us all.

## 123

## THE WISDOM IN A WHISPER

You didn't yell to make things heard, You always chose the softer word. A whispered truth, a knowing glance, A pause that gave the thought a chance.

And in those moments small and still, You taught me strength is not in will. But in the quiet way we speak— That wisdom lives in voices meek.

## 124

## YOU SHOWED ME HOW TO WAIT

When I was rushed to reach the end, You slowed me down and didn't bend. You said, "The good things take their time," And showed me patience is sublime.

You waited with a gentle hand, To help me learn and understand. That sometimes, strength is standing still— Not racing up the highest hill.

## 125

## THE WAY YOU HELD THE TRUTH

You didn't coat the world in gold, You let the honest stories unfold. You didn't lie to make it sweet— You showed me where the bitter meets.

But still, you gave me hope to cling— You held the truth like it had wings. So even when the world felt tough, You showed me truth could still be love.

## 126

## YOU LET ME BE AFRAID

You didn't say, "There's nothing there," You held my hand through every scare. You let me tremble, let me speak, You didn't call my worry weak.

And in your arms, I learned to face The fears that time could not erase. Not by denial or command— But with a steady, open hand.

## 127

## YOU MADE THE RULES FEEL WARM

The rules you gave weren't cold or bare, They wrapped around me like a prayer. Not meant to trap or shut me in— But guard my heart from things called "sin."

You didn't yell, or cage, or bind— But taught with love, not fear or mind. So now I build my world the same— With fences named in love's sweet name.

## 128

## YOU TAUGHT ME TO BELIEVE

You saw the spark when I could not, And held the faith that I forgot. You whispered dreams I hadn't dreamed, And planted hope where none had gleamed.

You didn't ask the world to bend— You just believed I'd find the end. And now when doubts surround my view, I hear the faith I learned from you.

## 129

## THE LESSONS IN YOUR LAUGHTER

You laughed at things that didn't go right, You turned mistakes into delight. You made it fine to try and fall— And still find joy inside it all.

Your laughter wasn't just for fun— It taught me how to face what's done. That even in the worst of days, A smile can soften sharpest haze.

## 130

## HOW YOU HANDLED LOSS

You let the tears fall soft and slow, You didn't fake or try to show. You let me see that pain was real, And crying too could help us heal.

But still you stood, with quiet grace, And didn't let the grief erase. You held the sorrow, strong and wise— And let me grieve through open eyes.

## 131

## YOU DIDN'T NEED TO BE PERFECT

You stumbled too, you missed a cue, And sometimes didn't have a clue. But in your flaws, I found what's true— That love is raw and real, not new.

You said, "I'm learning," just like me, You didn't fake who I should be. You showed me strong could still be scarred— And every lesson loved and shared.

## 132

## YOU TAUGHT ME WHEN TO REST

You made the bed with care each night, And said that sleep would set things right. You didn't chase the endless pace— You carved out peace in time and space.

You showed me work was not the prize, If joy was hidden from my eyes. Now when I pause, I hear your voice— That resting too is a brave choice.

## 133

## YOU TAUGHT ME TO BEGIN AGAIN

You let me fail, then try anew, And never said, "I'm done with you." You wiped the slate, reset the tone— And showed me how to stand alone.

You taught me life won't always flow, But starting fresh is how we grow. Now every time I fall or bend— I hear, "You can begin again."

## 134

# THE VALUE OF A PROMISE

You never broke your word to me, No matter how the world would be. If you said yes, it stayed that way— Your promises did not decay.

And so I learned, with every vow, That words mean something then and now. To stand by what we say or do— That lesson, Mom, I learned from you.

## 135

## HOW TO STAND ALONE

You didn't teach me just to lean, But how to walk when life turned mean. You showed me strength without a crowd, A quiet heart, both strong and proud.

You stood apart and stood up tall, And taught me not to fear the fall. Alone, you said, does not mean small— It means you know you've given all.

## 136

## THE BEAUTY OF ENOUGH

You didn't need the newest thing, Or shiny clothes or diamond ring. You found the joy in what you had, And turned the small into the glad.

You taught me rich was not in gold, But in the hearts we gently hold. And now I find, in all I do— Enough begins and ends with you.

## 137

## YOU LET ME SEE YOU CRY

You let your tears fall now and then, Not hidden from my eyes again. You didn't say, "Be strong, don't feel," You let the broken places heal.

You cried and taught me that was fine— That tears could cleanse, like softened wine. I hold that truth and pass it on— That crying too can make us strong.

# 138

## LESSONS IN THE LEAVING

You showed me love when you were near, But also in the way you'd clear— The space for me to find my way, And learn to walk my own each day.

You didn't clutch, you didn't cling, You let my life become its thing. And now I know what love can be— A lesson, and a letting be.

## 139

## LESSONS OF THE HEART

You taught me kindness, how to care, To lift the burdens others bear. With every word, your wisdom shines, A love that grows, a bond that binds.

Through lessons pure, my soul takes flight, Guided always by your light.

## 140

## THE SEEDS YOU'VE SOWN

With patient hands, you've sown the seeds, Of strength, of love, and noble deeds. Each tender lesson, softly told, A gift more precious than pure gold.

Your words, a beacon, bright and true, A mother's light that guides us through.

## 141

## THE WISDOM YOU GIVE

Your voice, a song of truth and care, Has taught me how to always share. Each word of wisdom, tried and true, A guiding star in skies so blue.

Your lessons linger, pure and strong, A melody that lasts lifelong.

## 142

# THE PATH YOU'VE SHOWN

You've shown the path with steps so sure, Through every challenge, you endure. Your steady hand, your knowing gaze, Have lit my world in countless ways.

With every lesson, strong and bright, You've brought me closer to the light.

## 143

## YOUR GENTLE ADVICE

Your gentle words, a soothing guide, Through life's vast storm, through shifting tide. Each piece of wisdom, softly said, A light to which my soul is led.

Your counsel, pure as morning dew, A gift that keeps my heart renewed.

## 144

## THE STRENGTH YOU TEACH

You teach me strength through every test, To always give my very best. With courage bold and heart so true, You've taught me all I need to do.

Your lessons, etched in time, remain, A source of joy, a shield from pain.

## 145

## THE WAY TO DREAM

You taught me how to reach for stars, To venture far and break through bars. Your wisdom gives my spirit wings, To strive for all that dreaming brings.

A mother's gift, so pure and rare, The way to dream, beyond compare.

## 146

## THROUGH EVERY WORD

Each word you speak, a gift to me, A window to what life can be. You teach with kindness, love, and care, A wisdom deep, beyond compare.

Your lessons linger, strong and true, A guiding light in all I do.

## 147

## THE TRUTH YOU SHARE

You share the truth with open eyes, To teach the world, to make me wise. Your honesty, a steadfast guide, Through every wave, through every tide.

Your lessons, clear as skies above, Have shown me life, and taught me love.

## 148

## THE LIGHT YOU BRING

You bring the light to darkest days, A mother's heart in countless ways. Through every lesson, love remains, A beacon bright through joys and pains.

Your wisdom shines, a gift to be, A guiding star that set me free.

## 149

## THE COURAGE TO LEARN

You've taught me courage, how to stand, To reach for dreams with steady hand. Your lessons guide my every choice, With love so pure, with steadfast voice.

Your wisdom, vast as skies so wide, Will always be my constant guide.

## 150

## A MOTHER'S TEACHINGS

A mother's words, a sacred song, That teaches right, that rights the wrong. Through every trial, joy, and care, Your wisdom lingers, always there.

Each lesson cherished, pure and true, A legacy passed down by you.

## 151

## THE WISDOM OF TIME

Through time, your wisdom stays the same, A guiding voice, a constant flame. With every word, with every deed, You've given all my heart could need.

Your lessons linger, pure and kind, A mother's love, a gift divine.

## PART V

# TRYING AGAIN

Life is full of challenges, and this section celebrates the resilience and determination that mothers inspire in us. **Trying Again** is a heartfelt tribute to the moments when we falter and the encouragement mothers provide to help us rise once more.

This section explores the unwavering support and belief mothers offer through touching poems, reminding us that failure is not the end but a stepping stone to success. It reflects on the courage and hope mothers instill, teaching us to keep going, persevere, and find strength in adversity.

These verses honor the incredible way mothers motivate us to try repeatedly, no matter the obstacles. They remind us that a mother's love and encouragement are often the driving forces behind our greatest triumphs.

## 152

## WHEN I WANTED TO QUIT

I said, "I can't," and dropped my head, You knelt beside me there instead. You didn't fix or force or preach— You whispered truths just out of reach.

You told me falling wasn't wrong, But staying down would take me long. And so I stood, though weak and torn— On words you planted, soft and warm.

## 153

## THE SECOND TRY

You never scolded when I failed, Or marked the times my courage paled. You simply smiled and said, "Again," And handed back the pad or pen.

You didn't shame the first mistake, You helped me see what love could make. That trying twice, and maybe three— Could still shape all I'm meant to be.

## 154

## YOU LET ME MESS IT UP

You gave me space to choose the wrong, To learn where I did not belong. You didn't hover close or tight— You let me stumble toward the right.

And when I came back bruised and bare, You didn't say, "I told you," there. You simply held me, soft and wide— And let the lesson swell with pride.

## 155

## THE COURAGE IN A MORNING

You said, "Each sunrise makes us new," No matter what the night's been through. You brewed the coffee, made the bed— And started hope with jam and bread.

You made me see that giving in Could end right where new dreams begin. And morning, in your voice and tone, Was where I learned I'm not alone.

## 156

## YOU DIDN'T KEEP SCORE

You never tallied all my wrongs, Or asked how long the hurt belongs. You wiped the slate, again, again— As if my past could never win.

You taught me grace through daily acts, Through second chances, loving pacts. And now I know what mercy's for— You gave your love, but kept no score.

## 157

## WHEN YOU PICKED ME UP AGAIN

You caught me when the world grew wild, And held me like your younger child. Though I was grown, and full of fight, You didn't leave me to the night.

You brushed my tears without a name, And said, "You're more than what you claim." You picked me up with quiet might— And helped me see my shattered light.

## 158

## THE STRENGTH IN SOFT REPEATS

You said, "Try once more," not loud, but low, Like streams that taught the rocks to grow. Your words weren't sharp, your hands weren't stern— You trusted I would rise and learn.

Each failure met your steady tone, Like wind that smooths the jagged stone. And now I rise with gentler feet— Because you stayed through soft repeats.

## 159

## YOU BELIEVED BEYOND MY VOICE

When I said, "No," or "Not this time," You saw beneath the stifled climb. You heard the hope I dared not name, And loved the spark that hid in shame.

You held the dreams I tried to leave, And whispered, "Daughter, still believe." You saw the try I couldn't show—And helped me find my fire below.

## 160

## YOU LET ME START AGAIN

You didn't say, "That's it, you're done," When all my chances came undone. You said, "So what? Just start once more," And opened wide another door.

You made mistakes feel less like ends, But like a path that always bends. And now I turn, and try anew— Because that's what I saw in you.

## 161

## YOU NEVER SAID, 'I TOLD YOU SO'

When I was wrong and knew it well, You never rang the judgment bell. You simply stood and held my hand, And helped me slowly understand.

You didn't mock, you didn't gloat, You wrapped regret in love's warm coat. And every time I fell below— You rose with me, and let me grow.

## 162

# THE PATIENCE YOU HAD FOR ME

You didn't rush the pace I took, You let me pause and take a look. While others pushed and pulled and cried, You simply stayed and stood beside.

When I would stop or turn around, You never sighed or made a sound. Your love became the quiet space Where I could fall and still find grace.

## 163

## YOU TAUGHT ME TO BEGIN SMALL

You said, "Don't try to leap too wide, Just take the next step, side by side." When I was lost in goals too grand, You gently placed one in my hand.

You showed me that a single spark Can light the corners of the dark. And in your calm and steady call, You taught me how to start things small.

# 164

# WHEN YOU WAITED THROUGH MY STORM

You didn't try to chase the rain, Or shield me from my growing pain. You let me shout, you let me burn— And knew, in time, that I would turn.

You didn't leave, you didn't flee, You stood like roots beneath a tree. And when I cracked from inner strife, You watered me with love and life.

## 165

## THE WAY YOU LET ME TRY AGAIN

You didn't say, "It's done, it's through," You only said, "I still trust you." No scoreboard kept, no shameful glance— Just wide, unspoken second chance.

You gave me space to miss the mark, To walk through both the light and dark. And when I rose, unsure and new— Your arms said, "This is trying, too."

## 166

## YOU BELIEVED BEFORE I DID

Before I saw the path ahead, You held the vision in your stead. You named the strength I couldn't see, And held it safely just for me.

While I was lost inside my doubt, You never let my flame go out. You kept it lit, a tiny spark— A lighthouse in my inner dark.

## 167

## THE FAILURES YOU CALLED BRAVE

You called me brave when I felt small, When all I did was trip and fall. You said the try was what you loved, Not just the win or prize dreamed of.

And in that view, I found my way— To rise again, to face the day. To fail with heart and not with shame— Because you praised the very aim.

## 168

# THE RESET YOU GAVE ME

When I had burned my bridges low, And didn't know where else to go, You didn't judge, or say, "Too late," You simply met me at the gate.

You made the past a folded sheet, And gave my future brand new feet. You didn't lecture, didn't preach— You handed me a softer reach.

## 169

## YOU DIDN'T SAY, 'BE STRONG'

You never asked me not to cry, You didn't say, "Just rise and try." You let me break, you let me bend, And met me like a trusted friend.

Then once the storm began to clear, You whispered strength into my ear. You didn't force a strength to wear— You helped me build it from despair.

## 170

## YOU TAUGHT ME HOW TO START OVER

You didn't rush my healing pace, Or wipe my tears with false embrace. You let me learn that loss was real— But didn't mean I couldn't heal.

You showed me how to build again, With fewer fears and wiser pen. And every time I had to part— You helped me choose a braver start.

## 171

## YOUR LOVE WAS A BRIDGE

When I had burned the road behind, And shame had nearly closed my mind, You built a bridge across my pain— With nothing asked, no debt, no chain.

You laid it stone by stone with grace, And met me in my broken place. And now I walk with steady pace— Because you gave me one more space.

## 172

## THE DAYS YOU LET ME REST

You didn't ask me to be tough, When life already felt too rough. You let me lie, you let me stay, And held the world a step away.

You knew that healing isn't fast, That strength still needs a place to last. And in your stillness, soft and wide, You let me rest, then rise with pride.

## 173

## YOU SHOWED ME I WAS MORE

When all I saw were broken things, You still believed I could grow wings. You didn't see the mess I made— You saw the light that didn't fade.

You saw the fire inside my doubt, And helped me let the ashes out. You gave me back what I had lost— You knew I still was worth the cost.

## 174

# THE LONG WAY WAS OKAY

You never rushed me down the path, Or mocked the turns that stirred your wrath. You didn't say, "You're late, you're slow,"— You smiled and said, "Just go and grow."

You made the long road feel just right, With every wrong still holding light. And now I walk at my own pace— Because you walked with patient grace.

## 175

## YOU CALLED ME HOME AGAIN

I wandered far from where I'd been, Ashamed of what I'd kept within. But when I knocked with trembling hand, You met me there and didn't stand.

You didn't ask for tales or proof, You let your silence speak the truth. And with a hug that held my shame— You called me home, and used my name.

## 176

## YOUR FAITH NEVER LEFT

Though I had failed and turned away, You never let your faith decay. You held it like a steady flame, Still whispering my truest name.

And when I couldn't meet your eyes, You met me under softer skies. You didn't boast, you didn't shout— You simply loved the doubt right out.

## 177

## GOLDEN DAYS

Golden days when joy was near, Your laughter rang for all to hear. Through little moments, pure and bright, You filled my world with love's own light.

Each memory blooms, a timeless hue, A treasure shared by me and you.

## 178

## A MEMORY'S TOUCH

The touch of your hand, a whisper so sweet, A moment of love where hearts always meet. Through time's vast journey, your care remains, A memory's touch that soothes and sustains.

Each fleeting glimpse, each tender thought, A mother's love, forever sought.

## 179

## THE STORIES WE SHARE

Your tales of wonder, soft and sweet, A joy in life none can defeat. Through every word, you paint the skies, With love so bright, it never dies.

Each story shared, a bond we keep, A treasure vast, a joy so deep.

## 180

## MOMENTS OF MAGIC

The magic found in everyday things, The joy you bring, the song life sings. Each glance, each smile, a moment rare, With you, life's filled with love and care.

These memories bloom, a precious hue, A tapestry woven by me and you.

## 181

## A MOTHER'S SMILE

Your smile could chase the clouds away, It turned the darkest night to day. Through every moment, great and small, Your joy became the best of all.

A mother's smile, so warm, so kind, A memory treasured in my mind.

## 182

## A MEMORY TO KEEP

A memory keeps the heart alive, Through all the years, it will survive. Each hug, each laugh, a tender thread, A bond of love, forever spread.

With every thought, you are right here, A memory kept, forever near.

## 183

## THE FIRST I RECALL

The first I recall, your gentle care, The way your love was always there. Through moments soft, through days so bright, You filled my world with endless light.

A mother's love, a perfect start, Forever cherished in my heart.

## 184

## A GLIMPSE OF THE PAST

A glimpse of the past, your face so kind, A memory etched within my mind. Through every moment, soft and true, Your love remains in all I do.

A mother's touch, a constant flame, A source of joy I can't explain.

## PART VI

# GROWTH AND SUPPORT:

Mothers are a source of unwavering encouragement, guiding us to become the best versions of ourselves. **Growth and Support** celebrate mothers' empowering role in nurturing confidence, fostering independence, and helping us flourish through life's challenges.

This section, through tender and uplifting poems, reflects on how mothers provide strength and assurance, cheering us on through successes and setbacks. It honors their ability to inspire personal growth while offering a safety net of unconditional love and understanding.

These verses highlight the profound impact of a mother's guidance, showing how her support helps us rise, thrive, and achieve our dreams.

## 185

## YOU KNEW I'D FIND MY WAY

You didn't chase me when I strayed, But trusted in the roots you laid. You knew the road would twist and pull, And still, your love was always full.

You didn't fear the days apart— You placed your hope inside my heart. And sure enough, through fear and gray, I found you waiting on the way.

## 186

## YOU LET ME START AT ZERO

You didn't scoff when I returned With empty hands and lessons learned. You made the start feel soft and wide, No shame, no pride you had to hide.

You said, "We all begin again," And smiled like I was always kin. You let me start from where I stood— And made me feel like I still could.

## 187

## YOU DIDN'T SAY, 'I KNEW'

You didn't say, "I told you so," When life had brought me far below. You held me close and kissed my cheek, And let my tired spirit speak.

You never used your truth to win— You let compassion lead again. And every word you didn't say Helped guide me back a softer way.

## 188

# THE GRACE YOU GAVE ME

You gave me grace in moments raw, Before the world could find its flaw. You didn't look with jaded eyes— You saw through hurt and heard the cries.

You didn't judge the choices made, But wrapped them in a lighter shade. And now I walk with fewer chains— Because your grace still softly reigns.

## 189

## YOU BELIEVED IN THE RISE

You didn't fear how far I fell, You knew the end would turn out well. You said, "It's never too far gone— There's always light before the dawn."

And sure enough, the morning came, And I stood taller, not the same. Because you saw beneath the cries— And only ever watched the rise.

## 190

# YOU LET ME FIND MY PACE

You never pushed me up the hill, Or told me when to just sit still. You watched me wander, fall, and climb— And trusted I would find my time.

You didn't map each twist or turn, Or lecture when I'd crash and burn. Instead, you waited, soft and wide, And kept your door and heart open wide.

And now I walk without the race— Because you let me find my pace.

## 191

## YOU LOVED ME AT MY WORST

You didn't flinch when I was cold, When all my kindness had been sold. You didn't beg for something more— You simply stood beside my door.

You let me grow through broken things, Through shattered dreams and missing wings. And still you loved with no request— You held my heart inside your chest.

I learned that love is not rehearsed— Because you loved me at my worst.

## 192

# YOU GAVE ME TIME TO MEND

You didn't rush the healing through, Or paint the pain in brighter hue. You let me sit, you let me cry, And didn't ask me how or why.

You held the space where wounds could breathe, And told me time was mine to sheathe. You didn't try to stitch too fast — You knew that mending had to last.

And when I rose, you didn't bend— You simply whispered, "Now you mend."

## 193

## YOU SAW BEYOND THE MESS

You didn't see the things I broke, The scattered dreams, the things I spoke. You saw beneath the flawed facade— The softer truth, the heart unflawed.

You didn't measure me by fall, But by the way I stood through all. You saw a light behind the blur— And called it back with love so sure.

You saw the more I can't express— You saw beyond my broken mess.

## 194

# YOU LET ME KEEP MY VOICE

You didn't hush me when I roared, Or beg for peace when tempers soared. You let me speak in every tone, And still reminded, "You're not alone."

You taught me how to shape my say, With words that clear and hearts that stay. And now I speak with thoughtful care— Because your calm was always there.

You never silenced noise or noise— You let me keep my sacred voice.

## 195

## THE ROOM YOU NEVER CLOSED

You never shut the door on me, No matter who I chose to be. Even when I strayed too far, You kept the porch light like a star.

You didn't chase or beg or plead, You simply waited, met my need. And when I came with aching eyes— You met me with a no-surprise.

I found my way to love exposed— Because you left no doorway closed.

## 196

# THE TRIES YOU COUNTED MOST

You didn't cheer for just the win, But for the heart I held within. You clapped the loudest when I tried— Even when I lost my pride.

You didn't care for score or fame, You saw the courage in the game. And every fall became a feat— Because your praise was still so sweet.

You made me strong, from coast to coast— By counting all the tries the most.

## 197

# YOU LET ME FALL WITH GRACE

You didn't rush to break the fall, Or wrap the world in cotton wall. You let me trip, you let me slide— And stayed in reach, but not inside.

You trusted I would find my feet, Though gravity felt dark and deep. You gave me space and let me learn— That grace is something I must earn.

And when I rose with dirt-stained face— You smiled and whispered, "That was grace."

## 198

## YOU HELPED ME BREATHE AGAIN

When panic made my vision blur, You held me close without a word. You didn't fix, you didn't flee— You stayed until I found my "me."

You taught me breath could be a guide, A bridge that fear could not divide. You held the silence soft and true— And I found strength by leaning through.

Now when I shake or lose my frame— I breathe, and softly speak your name.

# 199

## YOU LET ME LOVE MYSELF AGAIN

When I forgot my worth and name, You didn't meet me with your blame. You didn't point to what I lost— You offered love without the cost.

You wrapped me in a gentle tone, That said, "You're never quite alone." And though I doubted who I'd been— You let me love myself again.

Because you saw through pain and doubt— And showed me how to let me out.

## 200

# THE STEPS YOU TOOK BESIDE ME

You didn't lead or walk ahead, You took the path I feared instead. And matched your pace with every pause— No rush, no push, no scolding cause.

You made the road feel less alone, By walking where I found my own. You took each step with open grace— So I could find my sacred place.

Now every move I try to make— I think of steps you chose to take.

## 201

## YOU LET ME OWN THE PAIN

You didn't try to pull me out, Or sweep away my fear and doubt. You let me sit with what I felt— And let the ache be slowly dealt.

You let the silence take its place, Without a mask or hasty pace. And from that space, I came to see— That healing had to start with me.

You didn't fix what broke in rain— You let me fully own my pain.

## 202

## YOU CHEERED FOR MY RETURN

When I came back with lowered head, You didn't ask what I had said. You didn't dig or search for why— You only met me with a sigh.

A sigh that whispered, "You are home," No matter where my feet had roamed. You didn't weigh the time I'd gone— You only smiled and carried on.

And in your arms, I came to learn— There's always love inside return.

## 203

# YOU BELIEVED IN WHAT COULD BE

You saw beyond the now and here, Beyond my grief, beyond my fear. You held a vision I could trust— A dream unshaken by the dust.

You didn't speak in lofty terms, But planted hope like sleeping germs. And though I saw a broken me— You still believed in what could be.

That simple gift, your sacred view— Became the strength that pulled me through.

## 204

## YOU NEVER CALLED ME LOST

Though I had wandered far from right, You never said I'd left the light. You left the door just slightly cracked— And kept the porch lamp glowing back.

You let me find my way through pain, And never tightened guilt's old chain. And when I came, unsure and tossed— You said I'd never once been lost.

That grace you gave without the cost— Is love that will not count the lost.

## 205

## YOU LET ME TELL MY TRUTH

You didn't flinch or turn away, When I had things I had to say. You didn't interrupt or cry— You simply met my heavy sigh.

You let me speak without a mask, Without a test, without a task. And in that space, I found the proof— That love begins with simple truth.

And now, with all I hold in youth— I give the world what you called truth.

## 206

# THE TRY THAT TOOK TEN TIMES

You didn't care how many tries I needed just to realize. You watched me fail, and fall, and fight— And still you saw the flicker's light.

You counted effort, not success— And cleaned me up from each new mess. And when I finally met the climb— You said, "Some things just take their time."

You made me proud of every line— Of trying ten times, just for mine.

## 207

# THE FORGIVENESS YOU GAVE FIRST

Before I said a single word, You softened all the pain you heard. You let me offer broken speech— And met my failings out of reach.

You didn't hold it in your chest, You didn't make me pass a test. Forgiveness wasn't begged or burst— You always gave it to me first.

And now I know what peace is worth— Because you gave me back my worth.

## 208

## THE QUIET IN YOUR YES

You didn't need a big display, You nodded gently, led the way. Your "yes" was soft, without a boast— But somehow meant you loved me most.

You gave without a loud parade, You showed me how real love is made. Not by the words or loud success— But by the quiet in your "yes."

And every time I've felt alone— That quiet "yes" has brought me home.

## 209

# YOU NEVER SAID, 'TOO LATE'

You never said the time was gone, Or that my chance had moved along. You let me learn, you let me stall— And still believed I'd find it all.

You said, "Too late" is not a line, But just a fear we plant in time. And every time I showed up late— You smiled and said, "There's still a gate."

And in that space, I changed my fate— Because you never said, "Too late."

## 210

## A MOTHER'S GIFT

You've given more than words can say, A strength that grows in every way. With constant care and endless light, You've shaped my world and made it bright.

Each moment shared, your love inspires, A mother's gift that never tires.

## 211

## THROUGH GENTLE HANDS

With gentle hands, you taught me well, Through each success, through every fell. Your patience soft, your guidance pure, Have helped me grow and now endure.

Each step I take, your love leads me, A steady flame, a legacy.

## 212

## THE CARE YOU SHOW

You show me care through every deed, You give your heart for every need. Your guidance leads me through the night, Your wisdom fills the world with light.

With every step, with every call, Your love has always stood so tall.

# PART VII

# CULTURAL AND GENERATIONAL TIES

Mothers are the keepers of tradition, the bridges that connect generations, and the anchors of family heritage. **Cultural and Generational Ties** pay homage to their role in preserving the values, customs, and stories that define who we are.

Through thoughtful poems, this section explores how mothers pass down history, instill cultural pride, and strengthen the bonds that tie families together. It celebrates mothers' unique role in linking the past to the present and ensuring that the wisdom of our ancestors lives on through us.

These verses honor the traditions, rituals, and love that mothers carry forward. They are the heart of our shared history and the foundation of the legacies we leave behind.

## 213

## YOU HELPED ME TRUST MYSELF

You didn't question every choice, Or speak above my shaking voice. You let me learn by being free— To choose, to fail, to simply be.

You gave me tools but not control, You gave me room to shape my soul. And now I walk through wrong and right— Still trusting in my inner light.

Because you stood with love and stealth— I learned to truly trust myself.

## 214

# THE GROWTH YOU LET ME CLAIM

You didn't take the credit due, When I became someone brand new. You didn't say, "That came from me"— You let me own my destiny.

You never made the story yours, You let me open all the doors. And though your hand was always near— You let me rise without your steer.

The path I took, the rising flame— You let me walk and claim the name.

## 215

# YOU GAVE, THEN GAVE SOME MORE

You gave before I knew to ask, And never needed thanks or task. You gave in ways both loud and low— In silent nights and steady flow.

You gave your time, your dreams, your youth, You gave me love, you gave me truth. And even when your hands felt sore — You gave, and then you gave some more.

No gift could match what came before— The grace you gave, then gave once more.

## 216

## THE WAY YOU HELD MY LIGHT

You saw my light when it was small, When others didn't see at all. You cupped your hands around the glow, And whispered, "Let the brightness grow."

You didn't force it into fame, You simply spoke my sacred name. And now I shine without a fight— Because you helped me hold my light.

You fanned the flame through every night— You taught me how to hold my light.

## 217

## YOU GREW ME WITH YOUR LOVE

You didn't need to plant a seed, You simply met my every need. With every hug, with every glance, You gave my life its greatest chance.

You nurtured hope and shaped my view, And watered me in all I do. You were the sun, the rain, the ground— The reason I can bloom unbound.

I am because of what you gave— The love that made me strong and brave.

## 218

## THE STORIES THAT YOU TOLD

You didn't read from printed page, But passed down truth from age to age. With every tale, both soft and strong, You stitched our roots where they belong.

You made the past feel close and near, A voice that I could always hear. And now I hold those tales like gold— The legacy your stories told.

They echo deep, both proud and bold— The timeless truths you softly told.

## 219

## YOU TAUGHT ME WHERE I CAME FROM

You spoke of grandmas, lands, and songs, Of family ties and righting wrongs. You taught me names I'd never met— But ones my heart won't soon forget.

You showed me maps that weren't on walls, But lived inside ancestral calls. And now I stand, both proud and true— Because I came from all you knew.

You gave me roots that softly hum— You taught me where I came from.

## 220

## THE RECIPES YOU SHARED

You didn't cook from page or chart, You measured with your hands and heart. Each spice and stir, each simmered pot— Held more than taste—it held a lot.

You showed me how tradition stays, Through meals that warmed the hardest days. And now I cook with deeper care — Because your love still lingers there.

Your recipes became my prayer— Of culture passed from you to air.

## 221

## THE SONGS YOU USED TO SING

You sang me songs in lullaby, With notes that helped the dark go by. You didn't need a stage or mic— Your voice was soft and just the right.

You sang of joy, of grief, of grace, Of every age and every place. And now I hum those sacred tunes— Beneath the stars or under moons.

Your songs still make my spirit cling— To all the love your voice would bring.

## 222

## THE TRADITIONS THAT YOU KEPT

You kept the customs year by year, With laughter, food, and love sincere. You showed me what to pass along— What makes us proud, what keeps us strong.

From holidays to quiet days, You passed down warmth in quiet ways. And now I wear those truths like thread— They wrap around the life I've led.

Each custom that you softly swept— Remains a light you gently kept.

## 223

# YOU SPOKE THE LANGUAGE OF MY LINE

You taught me words not found in school, The tongue of grandmothers and rule. You didn't let the past erase— The rhythm in our native place.

You made me proud to speak with care, A language full of soul and prayer. Now every sound that leaves my voice— Feels rooted in a deeper choice.

You gave me words that now define— The sacred roots of every line.

## 224

# THE HEIRLOOMS THAT YOU SAVED

You kept the scarf, the ring, the vase— The things that time could not replace. You didn't hoard, you didn't hide— You held our past with loving pride.

You said, "These things are more than dust," "They're pieces of a sacred trust." And now I guard them, small but grand— Each one a torch passed hand to hand.

The things you saved now softly wave— The love in heirlooms that you gave.

## 225

# THE FAITH YOU PASSED TO ME

You didn't preach or force the way, You knelt and taught me how to pray. You showed me how belief can bloom— In silence, in the darkest room.

You shared a faith both wide and wise, That lived in hands and hopeful eyes. And though I've wandered, sought, and tried— Your steady faith still walks beside.

It wasn't pushed—it came for free— The sacred faith you passed to me.

## 226

## YOU MADE ME PART OF SOMETHING MORE

You made me feel I didn't stand Alone, but part of something grand. A tapestry of voice and name, A family line, a burning flame.

You tied me to the ones now gone, And helped me feel they still live on. And now I hold that banner high— A child beneath a boundless sky.

You gave me something to adore— You made me part of something more.

## 227

# THE LEGACY YOU LIVE THROUGH ME

Your life was not in lines and fame, But stitched in me—my soul, my name. You built a legacy so true— Through every little thing you do.

You passed it not through wealth or land, But by your ever-reaching hand. And now I walk with steady grace— Because your love still holds its place.

In all I am, in all I'll be— You live and breathe and rise through me.

## 228

## YOU WERE THE BRIDGE BETWEEN US ALL

You stood between the old and new, With wisdom deep and heart so true. You passed along what time once gave— And taught me how the strong behave.

You linked the past to where I stand, With gentleness and guiding hand. And now I see with clearer eyes— The bridge you built was strong and wise.

You were the one to heed the call— The bridge that stood between us all.

## 229

## THE WAY YOU HONORED THOSE BEFORE

You spoke their names with reverence wide, And kept their memory close with pride. You lit the candles, shared the song— And helped their legacy live long.

You made the past feel warm and near, Like every soul still lingers here. And now I speak their names aloud— And wear their love like woven shroud.

You showed me how to feel their lore— By how you honored those before.

## 230

## THE BLESSINGS IN YOUR EYES

You didn't bless with words alone, But in the way your love was shown. You looked at me, and I could tell— That I was known and loved as well.

No priest or prophet ever gave A blessing that could quite behave Like those you whispered with a glance— That turned each day into a chance.

I learned what holy truly implies— In all the blessings in your eyes.

## 231

## YOU MADE OUR HISTORY BEAUTIFUL

You told the tales that shaped our name, The trials passed, the quiet flame. You showed me how to read the pain— And still find strength in every chain.

You didn't hide the wounds or shame, But wrapped them in a sacred frame. You let me see both scar and shine— And know that every thread was mine.

You showed me truth, both hard and full— And made our history beautiful.

## 232

## YOU HELD THE WORLD IN RITUALS

The way you folded Sunday sheets, Or blessed the food before we'd eat— Was more than habit, more than time— It made our little acts sublime.

You lit the days with sacred flame, In tasks too small to earn a name. And now I keep them, one by one— The silent things that must be done.

Because your love wore daily jewels— You held the world in rituals.

## 233

## YOU SEWED OUR STORY INTO ME

In stitches, steps, and lullabies, You gave me more than soft replies. You gave me roots and room to roam— And left your story in my home.

You sewed it deep, beneath the skin, A quiet thread that hums within. And when I speak or walk or cry— I feel your fabric flutter by.

Your love, your name, your legacy— You sewed our story into me.

## 234

# THE WISDOM IN YOUR SILENCE

You didn't always speak your mind, But let the silence be refined. You taught me not to fill the space— But wait, and watch, and honor grace.

In pauses long and glances small, You taught me how to hear it all. And now I speak with softer tone— Because your silence made me grown.

Not every truth must claim defiance— You shaped my life with quiet science.

## 235

## YOU DANCED BETWEEN THE GENERATIONS

You held your mother's gentle way, And passed it down in what you'd say. You moved with rhythm, old and new— A bridge of lineage shining through.

You braided future with the past, And showed me love that's built to last. You danced through customs, rules, and more— Then taught me how to find the door.

With every turn and graceful move— You danced between what we must prove.

## 236

## YOU MADE TRADITION FEEL LIKE LOVE

It wasn't forced or cold or stern— But something warm I'd always learn. You tied the ribbon with a smile— And let me question for a while.

You taught that love could wear old shoes, That heritage could feel like hues. And now I keep those customs bright— Not out of rule, but sheer delight.

You didn't push or rise above— You made tradition feel like love.

## 237

## YOU GAVE ME TIME ITSELF

You gave me more than just your name, You gave me time without a claim. You spent your days, your dreams, your art — To pour yourself into my heart.

And now I walk with all you gave— Each sacrifice, each wave you brave. And when the hours pull me through— I think of time I owe to you.

You gifted more than wealth or pelf— You gave me life, you gave me self.

## 238

## THE THREAD OF GENERATIONS

You weave the thread from past to now, A mother's gift, a solemn vow. With every story, every song, You show us where we all belong.

Your love connects through time and space, A bond that nothing can erase.

## 239

## KEEPER OF TRADITIONS

You hold the customs close at heart, Ensuring they will never part. Through every ritual, tale, and rhyme, You carry culture through all time.

A mother's role, so bold, so true, Preserving what we hold in view.

## 240

## THE BRIDGE YOU BUILD

You build a bridge from then to now, With love, you teach us all the how. Each custom shared, each sacred rite, You pass along with heart's delight.

A legacy that will not fade, Through you, the past is softly laid.

## 241

## STORIES OF OLD

The stories of old you softly tell, Hold wisdom vast, a wishing well. Each word, a treasure, deep and rare, A gift of love beyond compare.

Through time, these tales have found their place, A mother's gift, a timeless grace.

## 242

## THE ROOTS THAT BIND

The roots you plant, both firm and deep, Through generations, still they keep. A tether strong to days gone by, A mother's love that cannot die.

You teach us where our hearts belong, Through culture's ties, both rich and strong.

## 243

## SONGS OF THE PAST

The songs you sing, so sweet, so clear, Remind us all that love is near. Through every note, through every tune, You guard the past like the shining moon.

A keeper of voices, melodies true, Preserving the world that once we knew.

## 244

## GENERATIONS' GUIDE

You guide us through the ages past, With wisdom deep and love that lasts. Through every custom, every care, You show the world how much you share.

A mother's touch, a guiding hand, A bond of love we understand.

## 245

## THE WISDOM YOU SHARE

Through every tale, through every rhyme, You carry forth the weight of time. A mother's care, a world of grace, Preserving culture's sacred place.

Each lesson taught, so firm, so true, A lasting legacy brought by you.

## 246

## ROOTS OF THE EARTH

From roots of the earth, you show the way, To honor the past and cherish today. Through ancient customs, softly told, You guard traditions, pure as gold.

Forever treasured, your care will be, A mother's love through history.

## 247

## ECHOES OF THE PAST

The echoes of the past still ring, Through every tale, through every thing. You hold the customs, firm and sure, A mother's love that will endure.

Through time, your care has made it last, A bond that ties us to the past.

# PART VIII

# BONUS POEMS

**To Moms,**

To the mothers whose lullabies softened the edges of sleepless nights... To the mothers whose strength stood steady when the world did not... To the mothers who gave without asking, who stayed without praise, and who loved in ways that words will never quite capture.

Whether you raised a village or just one soul, Whether your love came by birth, by choice, or by heart, You are the thread that holds generations together— The silent architect of hope, courage, and tomorrow.

These final poems are whispers of gratitude echoing across borders, cultures, and time.

Thank you for being the miracle in someone's story.

## 248

# YOU LIFTED WHEN I DOUBTED ME

When I believed I couldn't rise, You met me with unshaken eyes. You didn't tell me who to be— You only said, "I still see me."

You didn't force a script or plan, You simply reached and took my hand. And in that hold, I found the key— That you believed enough for me.

You were the voice that set me free— And lifted when I doubted me.

## 249

## THE WIND BENEATH MY START

You never tried to steal the light, Or lead my wings in your own flight. You didn't take the skies from me— You only made me want to be.

You stood behind, not out in front, And let me take the first big hunt. You gave my dreams a gentle start— And filled the sails behind my heart.

Your quiet strength became the art— Of being wind beneath my start.

## 250

# YOU SAW POTENTIAL IN MY PAIN

You didn't flinch when I was low, You said, "This too will help you grow." You made me see what pain could teach, Even when hope was out of reach.

You saw the roots beneath the rain, The chance inside the ache and strain. And in your arms, the loss felt kind— A softened truth for me to find.

You saw a bloom inside the strain— You saw potential in my pain.

## 251

## YOU LET ME TAKE THE LEAD

You didn't map out all the days, Or shape my life in rigid ways. You stood beside me with a smile, And let me lead for just a while.

You watched me turn and choose my pace, With every risk I tried to face. And when I asked, you gave your view— But only when I wanted you.

You gave me space to plant my seed— You loved enough to let me lead.

## 252

# THE APPLAUSE THAT SHAPED MY STRENGTH

You clapped when others didn't see, The small brave acts that strengthened me. You didn't wait for crowds to cheer— You made my courage loud and clear.

You noticed all the quiet wins, The daily tries, the little spins. And in your praise, I found the proof— That worth is not just measured truth.

You gave my steps their boldest length— With quiet praise that built my strength.

## 253

## YOU LET ME CHANGE MY MIND

You didn't say, "You said before," Or lock me in to plans I swore. You let me shift, explore the new, And grow in ways I never knew.

You gave me room to think again, To question, dream, restart, and then— To trust that change was not a shame, But just a new and truer name.

You let me choose, not be confined— You loved me as I changed my mind.

## 254

## YOU HELPED ME FACE THE MIRROR

You didn't hide the things I missed, Or sugarcoat with every kiss. You spoke the truth with gentle care, So I could grow and still feel fair.

You helped me see the parts I feared, The flaws I masked, the thoughts I smeared. But through it all, you held me near— So truth felt less like pain than clear.

You made me stronger year by year— By helping me face every mirror.

## 255

## YOU BELIEVED I'D FIND MY WAY

You didn't need a perfect plan, Or hold a rulebook in your hand. You trusted I would learn and grow— And find the things I had to know.

You didn't ask for step-by-step, You simply gave me love and depth. And with that love, I carved a way— Through all the storms that begged me stay.

You gave me faith that didn't sway— And trusted I'd find my own way.

## 256

## YOU BUILT ME BRICK BY BRICK

You didn't rush the walls I made, You laid them slowly, shade by shade. With every word, each choice you kept, You shaped the soul where dreams have slept.

You didn't hand me strength too fast, You knew that solid things must last. And every moment that we shared— Became the reason I've been spared.

You built me strong, with grit and stick— You built me steady, brick by brick.

## 257

# THE GROWTH YOU NEVER CLAIMED

You never pointed to your role, Or claimed the credit for my soul. You stood behind the bloom I grew, And smiled like it had naught to do with you.

But I could trace each leaf and vine Back to your hands, your heart, your spine. And now I see through clearer eyes— Your quiet touch beneath the rise.

You helped me climb and never named— The sacred growth you never claimed.

## 258

## YOU LET ME MAKE MISTAKES

You didn't flinch when I fell short, Or send my dreams to higher court. You let me fail and try once more— And never kept a closing door.

You gave me space to learn and bend, To see how growth and flaws can blend. You didn't rush to clean the slate— You let me fall, then helped me wait.

And in those cracks that my pain makes— You grew me strong through my mistakes.

## 259

## YOU STOOD BACK AND LET ME SHINE

You didn't reach to steal the light, Or make my moments yours by right. You clapped from just a step behind— With joy so rich, so rare, so kind.

You didn't crave a share of fame, Or press your presence on my name. Instead, you smiled and lit the way— Then let me rise into the day.

Your love was bright, but so divine— It stepped aside to let me shine.

## 260

# THE VOICE YOU PLANTED DEEP

You told me I was strong and wise, With magic deep behind my eyes. You whispered dreams into my bones— In quiet tones, like sacred tones.

And now when I feel small or stuck, Or low on faith, or short on luck— I hear your words, like morning rain, That wash me free from fear and strain.

You gave me roots, so I could leap— You planted courage nice and deep.

## 261

## YOU NEVER ASKED FOR PRAISE

You didn't beg for thanks or cheers, You gave your best through all the years. Not for a prize or loud acclaim— But just because you loved the same.

You poured your heart in silent ways, In meals, in rides, in busy days. And though you never asked for more— Your love still rings from shore to shore.

You showed me how pure love behaves— By giving, never asking praise.

## 262

# THE ROOTS THAT LET ME ROAM

You didn't tie me to the ground, Or lock me in where you were found. You raised me firm, with just enough— To walk alone when things got tough.

You gave me roots, but wings as well, To chase the stories I could tell. And now no matter where I go— Your steady roots still help me grow.

You gave me earth, and air, and dome— The kind of roots that let me roam.

## 263

## YOU LET ME OUTGROW YOU

You didn't cling when I outgrew The things we once would always do. You watched me change and stretch my form— And let me step beyond your norm.

You didn't shame my growing ways, Or try to hold me in old days. You loved me through my changing hue— And let me outgrow even you.

That kind of love is strong and true— To let me outgrow even you.

## 264

# THE PRIDE YOU NEVER SPOKE

You didn't shout the things you felt, Or wear your pride upon your belt. You let your joy stay soft and low— But somehow let your heart still show.

You beamed with pride in quiet ways, In folded notes and praise delays. And though you said it not aloud— I always felt your spirit proud.

I wore your love just like a cloak— Wrapped in the pride you never spoke.

## 265

## YOU LET ME LEARN MY VOICE

You let me say the words all wrong, And didn't rush to make them strong. You didn't shape each thought I shared— You simply sat, and gently cared.

You let me search through sounds and thought, And learn which truths were mine or not. And in your stillness, calm and true— My voice became a part of you.

I found myself in every choice— Because you let me learn my voice.

## 266

## YOU DIDN'T SAY 'BE BETTER'

You didn't say, "You must improve," You only helped my heart to move. You didn't list what I should do— You said, "I see the best in you."

You made me feel I could be more, Not from demand, but from your core. And slowly I became that girl— Who tried to shine and change the world.

You never said, "Be best or better"— You just became my quiet setter.

## 267

## YOU CARRIED ME IN SILENCE

You bore the weight I never knew, And held the tears I never drew. You kept the worries out of sight, And made my world feel warm and light.

You let me think I flew alone, While holding every stone you'd known. And now I see, through years and miles— You carried me with quiet smiles.

The strength I feel is not just mine— It echoes in your unseen spine.

## 268

## YOU BUILT MY QUIET STRENGTH

You didn't need to raise your voice, To teach me grace or give me choice. You showed me calm, you showed me still, And shaped my spine with steady will.

You didn't shout to be obeyed, You simply led the love you made. And now, in storms, I hold my ground— In silence where your roots are found.

You didn't push or fight or length— You built me up with quiet strength.

## 269

## YOU CHEERED FOR WHO I WAS

You didn't wish that I would change, Or shift my soul to fit some range. You loved me raw, you loved me true— With every shade and point of view.

You didn't ask me to pretend, Or shape myself to match a trend. You clapped for me without applause— Just proud of who I truly was.

You gave your cheer without a cause— You simply loved me, just because.

## 270

## THE LESSONS IN YOUR HANDS

Your hands were never just for chores, They opened dreams and unseen doors. They tied my shoes, they dried my tears, They built my courage through the years.

They soothed my brow, they brushed my hair, They taught me how to hope and care. And even now, with all I do— I feel those hands still guiding through.

Your touch still teaches where it lands— The stories live inside your hands.

## 271

## YOU LET ME CLIMB ALONE

You didn't lift me every time, But pointed toward the hill to climb. You let me stumble, let me start— And find the rhythm in my heart.

You didn't block the path with fear, You let me walk, then brought me near. And when I reached the top unsure— You clapped, and made my joy feel pure.

You gave me roots and stepping stone— And let me climb that hill alone.

# 272

# THE YES BENEATH THE NO

You said "no" when you had to stand, But held it with a loving hand. You didn't scold or shout or blame— You gave the "no" without the shame.

But underneath, your love still shined, A gentle yes within the kind. You told me "no" with so much care— I knew your heart was always there.

You taught me grace in ebb and flow— Even inside the word "no."

# 1

# CLOSING THOUGHTS

As we reach the final pages of **Whispers to Mom**, I invite you to reflect on our profound journey through poems that honor love, resilience, and the timeless bond of motherhood. These verses are more than words; they are expressions of gratitude, admiration, and connection. Each tributes to mothers' remarkable role in shaping lives and families across generations.

Through seven distinct sections, we have celebrated the miraculous beginnings, the quiet sacrifices, the joyful memories, and the wisdom that mothers impart. We have acknowledged their strength, nurturing spirit, and ability to preserve the threads of tradition that unite us all. Most importantly, we have celebrated the love transcending time—a constant, unwavering, and transformative love.

I hope this collection has resonated with you, evoking cherished memories and heartfelt gratitude for the mothers in your life. Whether you gift this book or keep it as a reminder of the bond you share, may it serve as a lasting testament to the beauty of motherhood.

Thank you to all the extraordinary women whose love leaves an indelible mark on the world. Your strength, grace, and care will forever be the foundation upon which lives are built.

With deepest appreciation,

A. Perkins

# 2

# INDEX OF POEMS

*For an Interactive Index of the Poems, click here.*

# INDEX LIST OF POEM

*Preface* — 15
*Introduction* — 17
*What Awaits You in These Pages* — 19

PART I
**FROM BIRTH TO BOND: A MOTHER'S LOVE**

1. The Moment You Arrived — 25
2. Through Tender Years — 26
3. The First Embrace — 27
4. When You Said My Name — 28
5. My First Teacher — 29
6. The Language of Touch — 30
7. Your Voice Was My First Song — 31
8. Morning Moments — 32
9. Held Without Asking — 33
10. You Named Me Twice — 34
11. A Mother's Hands — 35
12. The Blanket You Wove — 36
13. Through Fevered Nights — 37
14. The First Goodbye — 38
15. You Were My World — 39
16. The First Time You Prayed for Me — 40
17. A Cradle of Light — 41
18. The Songs You Made Up — 42
19. The Lessons in the Small Things — 43
20. Always the First to See — 44
21. The Moment You Arrived — 45
22. The Way You Looked at Me — 46
23. Through Tender Years — 47
24. The Strength You Showed — 48

| | |
|---|---|
| 25. Life's First Gift | 49 |
| 26. The Bond You Made | 50 |
| 27. A Thousand Lullabies | 51 |
| 28. Cradled in Love | 52 |
| 29. In the Quiet Moments | 53 |
| 30. Rocked in Your Arms | 54 |
| 31. The First Embrace | 55 |
| 32. Your Sacrifice | 56 |
| 33. Your Endless Love | 57 |
| 34. The Way You Watched Me Sleep | 58 |

PART II
## LOVE AND GRATITUDE:

| | |
|---|---|
| 35. A Heart That Gave Without Return | 61 |
| 36. Thank You for Staying | 62 |
| 37. I Didn't Know Then | 63 |
| 38. The Meals You Made | 64 |
| 39. A Quiet Thank You | 65 |
| 40. You Clapped the Loudest | 66 |
| 41. The Notes You Wrote | 67 |
| 42. I Know Now What It Cost | 68 |
| 43. Your Love Was Loud Without a Sound | 69 |
| 44. When I Forgot to Say It | 70 |
| 45. You Gave Me Your Mornings | 71 |
| 46. The Hands That Held My World | 72 |
| 47. A Thank You Left Unsaid | 73 |
| 48. Your Love Was in the Details | 74 |
| 49. When You Let Me Go | 75 |
| 50. All the Things I Never Noticed | 76 |
| 51. Your Voice Was Always Near | 77 |
| 52. I Know Now Why You Waited | 78 |
| 53. The Gifts You Didn't Wrap | 79 |
| 54. The Thank You in My Eyes | 80 |
| 55. The Strength Behind the Smile | 81 |
| 56. Carrying More Than You Shared | 82 |
| 57. The Sleepless Years | 83 |

| | |
|---|---|
| 58. The Fire in Your Fight | 84 |
| 59. You Broke So I Could Heal | 85 |
| 60. A Mother's Love | 86 |
| 61. The Heart That Always Knows | 87 |
| 62. Your Gentle Light | 88 |
| 63. The Bond You Build | 89 |
| 64. The Keeper of Dreams | 90 |
| 65. Forever Your Song | 91 |
| 66. Beacon of Love | 92 |
| 67. You Taught Me How | 93 |
| 68. Your Gentle Ways | 94 |
| 69. The Roots You Lay | 95 |
| 70. Radiant Soul | 96 |
| 71. You Are My Anchor | 97 |
| 72. Timeless Love | 98 |
| 73. Shelter from the Storm | 99 |
| 74. Unbreakable Bond | 100 |

PART III
## STRENGTH AND SACRIFICE

| | |
|---|---|
| 75. The Hands That Didn't Tremble | 103 |
| 76. The Day You Went Without | 104 |
| 77. Quiet Doesn't Mean Weak | 105 |
| 78. You Never Left the Room | 106 |
| 79. The Sacrifice I Never Saw | 107 |
| 80. You Loved Me Through the Hard Parts | 108 |
| 81. The Way You Softened Suffering | 109 |
| 82. The Cost of Loving Me | 110 |
| 83. The Day You Didn't Cry | 111 |
| 84. Your Patience Was My Shield | 112 |
| 85. You Hid Your Hurts | 113 |
| 86. You Chose Me Over Rest | 114 |
| 87. The Silence You Endured | 115 |
| 88. You Were the One Who Stayed | 116 |
| 89. The Fire in Your Quiet Ways | 117 |
| 90. You Taught Me Right from Wrong | 118 |

| | |
|---|---|
| 91. Lessons in the Little Things | 119 |
| 92. You Taught Me How to Speak | 120 |
| 93. How to Love and Let Go | 121 |
| 94. You Made Me Apologize | 122 |
| 95. The Truth in Your Eyes | 123 |
| 96. You Taught Me Grace in Failing | 124 |
| 97. How to Forgive | 125 |
| 98. What Matters Most | 126 |
| 99. You Taught Me to Be Me | 127 |
| 100. The Power You Bear | 128 |
| 101. Unseen Sacrifices | 129 |
| 102. Through Tireless Nights | 130 |
| 103. The Burden You Carry | 131 |
| 104. The Strength You Show | 132 |
| 105. A Shield of Love | 133 |
| 106. Your Quiet Resolve | 134 |
| 107. Your Endless Fight | 135 |
| 108. The Courage to Give | 136 |
| 109. The Weight You Bear | 137 |
| 110. Through Every Strife | 138 |
| 111. Strength Unseen | 139 |
| 112. Through Every Scar | 140 |
| 113. The Force You Are | 141 |

PART IV
**LIFE LESSONS**

| | |
|---|---|
| 114. The Power of Please and Thank You | 145 |
| 115. The Lessons Weren't in Books | 146 |
| 116. The Way You Handled Anger | 147 |
| 117. You Taught Me Time Was Gold | 148 |
| 118. You Showed Me How to Listen | 149 |
| 119. Lessons in Applause | 150 |
| 120. You Let Me Ask the Questions | 151 |
| 121. You Taught Me to Make Do | 152 |
| 122. How to Apologize with Grace | 153 |
| 123. The Wisdom in a Whisper | 154 |

| | | |
|---|---|---|
| 124. | You Showed Me How to Wait | 155 |
| 125. | The Way You Held the Truth | 156 |
| 126. | You Let Me Be Afraid | 157 |
| 127. | You Made the Rules Feel Warm | 158 |
| 128. | You Taught Me to Believe | 159 |
| 129. | The Lessons in Your Laughter | 160 |
| 130. | How You Handled Loss | 161 |
| 131. | You Didn't Need to Be Perfect | 162 |
| 132. | You Taught Me When to Rest | 163 |
| 133. | You Taught Me to Begin Again | 164 |
| 134. | The Value of a Promise | 165 |
| 135. | How to Stand Alone | 166 |
| 136. | The Beauty of Enough | 167 |
| 137. | You Let Me See You Cry | 168 |
| 138. | Lessons in the Leaving | 169 |
| 139. | Lessons of the Heart | 170 |
| 140. | The Seeds You've Sown | 171 |
| 141. | The Wisdom You Give | 172 |
| 142. | The Path You've Shown | 173 |
| 143. | Your Gentle Advice | 174 |
| 144. | The Strength You Teach | 175 |
| 145. | The Way to Dream | 176 |
| 146. | Through Every Word | 177 |
| 147. | The Truth You Share | 178 |
| 148. | The Light You Bring | 179 |
| 149. | The Courage to Learn | 180 |
| 150. | A Mother's Teachings | 181 |
| 151. | The Wisdom of Time | 182 |

PART V
**TRYING AGAIN**

| | | |
|---|---|---|
| 152. | When I Wanted to Quit | 185 |
| 153. | The Second Try | 186 |
| 154. | You Let Me Mess It Up | 187 |
| 155. | The Courage in a Morning | 188 |
| 156. | You Didn't Keep Score | 189 |

| | |
|---|---|
| 157. When You Picked Me Up Again | 190 |
| 158. The Strength in Soft Repeats | 191 |
| 159. You Believed Beyond My Voice | 192 |
| 160. You Let Me Start Again | 193 |
| 161. You Never Said, 'I Told You So' | 194 |
| 162. The Patience You Had for Me | 195 |
| 163. You Taught Me to Begin Small | 196 |
| 164. When You Waited Through My Storm | 197 |
| 165. The Way You Let Me Try Again | 198 |
| 166. You Believed Before I Did | 199 |
| 167. The Failures You Called Brave | 200 |
| 168. The Reset You Gave Me | 201 |
| 169. You Didn't Say, 'Be Strong' | 202 |
| 170. You Taught Me How to Start Over | 203 |
| 171. Your Love Was a Bridge | 204 |
| 172. The Days You Let Me Rest | 205 |
| 173. You Showed Me I Was More | 206 |
| 174. The Long Way Was Okay | 207 |
| 175. You Called Me Home Again | 208 |
| 176. Your Faith Never Left | 209 |
| 177. Golden Days | 210 |
| 178. A Memory's Touch | 211 |
| 179. The Stories We Share | 212 |
| 180. Moments of Magic | 213 |
| 181. A Mother's Smile | 214 |
| 182. A Memory to Keep | 215 |
| 183. The First I Recall | 216 |
| 184. A Glimpse of the Past | 217 |

PART VI
**GROWTH AND SUPPORT:**

| | |
|---|---|
| 185. You Knew I'd Find My Way | 221 |
| 186. You Let Me Start at Zero | 222 |
| 187. You Didn't Say, 'I Knew' | 223 |
| 188. The Grace You Gave Me | 224 |
| 189. You Believed in the Rise | 225 |

| | | |
|---|---|---|
| 190. | You Let Me Find My Pace | 226 |
| 191. | You Loved Me at My Worst | 227 |
| 192. | You Gave Me Time to Mend | 228 |
| 193. | You Saw Beyond the Mess | 229 |
| 194. | You Let Me Keep My Voice | 230 |
| 195. | The Room You Never Closed | 231 |
| 196. | The Tries You Counted Most | 232 |
| 197. | You Let Me Fall with Grace | 233 |
| 198. | You Helped Me Breathe Again | 234 |
| 199. | You Let Me Love Myself Again | 235 |
| 200. | The Steps You Took Beside Me | 236 |
| 201. | You Let Me Own the Pain | 237 |
| 202. | You Cheered for My Return | 238 |
| 203. | You Believed in What Could Be | 239 |
| 204. | You Never Called Me Lost | 240 |
| 205. | You Let Me Tell My Truth | 241 |
| 206. | The Try That Took Ten Times | 242 |
| 207. | The Forgiveness You Gave First | 243 |
| 208. | The Quiet in Your Yes | 244 |
| 209. | You Never Said, 'Too Late' | 245 |
| 210. | A Mother's Gift | 246 |
| 211. | Through Gentle Hands | 247 |
| 212. | The Care You Show | 248 |

PART VII
**CULTURAL AND GENERATIONAL TIES**

| | | |
|---|---|---|
| 213. | You Helped Me Trust Myself | 251 |
| 214. | The Growth You Let Me Claim | 252 |
| 215. | You Gave, Then Gave Some More | 253 |
| 216. | The Way You Held My Light | 254 |
| 217. | You Grew Me With Your Love | 255 |
| 218. | The Stories That You Told | 256 |
| 219. | You Taught Me Where I Came From | 257 |
| 220. | The Recipes You Shared | 258 |
| 221. | The Songs You Used to Sing | 259 |
| 222. | The Traditions That You Kept | 260 |

| | |
|---|---|
| 223. You Spoke the Language of My Line | 261 |
| 224. The Heirlooms That You Saved | 262 |
| 225. The Faith You Passed to Me | 263 |
| 226. You Made Me Part of Something More | 264 |
| 227. The Legacy You Live Through Me | 265 |
| 228. You Were the Bridge Between Us All | 266 |
| 229. The Way You Honored Those Before | 267 |
| 230. The Blessings in Your Eyes | 268 |
| 231. You Made Our History Beautiful | 269 |
| 232. You Held the World in Rituals | 270 |
| 233. You Sewed Our Story Into Me | 271 |
| 234. The Wisdom in Your Silence | 272 |
| 235. You Danced Between the Generations | 273 |
| 236. You Made Tradition Feel Like Love | 274 |
| 237. You Gave Me Time Itself | 275 |
| 238. The Thread of Generations | 276 |
| 239. Keeper of Traditions | 277 |
| 240. The Bridge You Build | 278 |
| 241. Stories of Old | 279 |
| 242. The Roots That Bind | 280 |
| 243. Songs of the Past | 281 |
| 244. Generations' Guide | 282 |
| 245. The Wisdom You Share | 283 |
| 246. Roots of the Earth | 284 |
| 247. Echoes of the Past | 285 |

PART VIII
**BONUS POEMS**

| | |
|---|---|
| 248. You Lifted When I Doubted Me | 289 |
| 249. The Wind Beneath My Start | 290 |
| 250. You Saw Potential in My Pain | 291 |
| 251. You Let Me Take the Lead | 292 |
| 252. The Applause That Shaped My Strength | 293 |
| 253. You Let Me Change My Mind | 294 |
| 254. You Helped Me Face the Mirror | 295 |
| 255. You Believed I'd Find My Way | 296 |

| | |
|---|---|
| 256. You Built Me Brick by Brick | 297 |
| 257. The Growth You Never Claimed | 298 |
| 258. You Let Me Make Mistakes | 299 |
| 259. You Stood Back and Let Me Shine | 300 |
| 260. The Voice You Planted Deep | 301 |
| 261. You Never Asked for Praise | 302 |
| 262. The Roots That Let Me Roam | 303 |
| 263. You Let Me Outgrow You | 304 |
| 264. The Pride You Never Spoke | 305 |
| 265. You Let Me Learn My Voice | 306 |
| 266. You Didn't Say 'Be Better' | 307 |
| 267. You Carried Me in Silence | 308 |
| 268. You Built My Quiet Strength | 309 |
| 269. You Cheered for Who I Was | 310 |
| 270. The Lessons in Your Hands | 311 |
| 271. You Let Me Climb Alone | 312 |
| 272. The Yes Beneath the No | 313 |
| 1. Closing Thoughts | 315 |
| 2. Index of Poems | 317 |
| 3. Author's Note | 328 |
| 4. About the Author | 330 |

# 3

# AUTHOR'S NOTE

This book is more than a collection of poems; it is a love letter to the women who shape our world in profound and countless ways—our mothers. Writing **Whispers to Mom** has been a reflection, gratitude, and celebration journey. Each verse is inspired by the universal experiences of love, resilience, and the tender bonds that define motherhood.

As I wrote these poems, I thought about the sacrifices mothers make, the wisdom they share, and the strength they embody. But I also thought about the small, quiet moments—the laughter, the gentle touch, the way they light up our lives with their presence. These are the moments I hope this book captures, and these are the moments I hope you'll reflect on as you read it.

To anyone who picks up this book, I hope it will serve as a bridge—connecting you to the memories, lessons, and love

*Author's Note*

you share with your mother. And for those who wish to gift this book to their mothers, I hope it becomes a keepsake, a treasure they will cherish for years.

Thank you for allowing me to share your journey through these pages. This is my whisper to all mothers and my way of honoring the extraordinary women we hold dear.

With gratitude,

A. Perkins

# 4

# ABOUT THE AUTHOR

A. Perkins embodies resilience and determination. Born in Morehead, Mississippi, to a single mother with a third-grade education, A. Perkins is a fifth-generation survivor of slavery raised in East Saint Louis, Illinois—one of America's toughest areas. Despite these challenging circumstances, his early accomplishments were exceptional.

A. Perkins married at 18, with his wife just 16, and together, they juggled several jobs, working tirelessly to move their family out of the ghetto. A. Perkins finished high school at night school and graduated from SIU-Edwardsville through college work-study. Tragically, his mother, who had eight children, died suddenly at 42, but A. Perkins' resilience only grew stronger.

A. Perkins' determination and focus were evident as he graduated from college in three years despite his obstacles. At 23,

## About the Author

he and his young wife adopted his two younger brothers and sister, showcasing his caring nature. A. Perkins became one of the first people of color from East Saint Louis to graduate from college and attend Air Force Officer Training, marking a significant educational achievement.

A. Perkins' life is a testament to his diverse talents and experiences. He holds an MBA from the University of North Dakota. He is an author, poet, former nuclear missile launch officer, decorated Air Force Officer previously assigned to the Pentagon, and a 100% disabled veteran. A. Perkins is also an entrepreneur, former CEO of a small public company that achieved a significant dollar market cap, teacher, technologist, writer, art dealer, world traveler, and former resident of Spain and China. In addition, he is a devoted husband, father, grandfather, brother, son, former prisoner, felon, and a true trailblazer. His life is a fascinating journey of exploration and achievement.

A. Perkins' personal life is a testament to the love and support he has received. He is married to his beautiful wife, who he met in China, and has two outstanding daughters and a remarkable son. They also have several grandchildren, nieces, nephews, and other family members who are a constant source of joy and inspiration. Their unwavering support has guided A. Perkins' life, filling it with warmth and love.

Made in United States
Orlando, FL
05 May 2025